EVERYDAY CATHOLIC

Prayer

EVERYDAY CATHOLIC

Prayer

A LITTLE OFFICE BOOK

Angela Tilby

PARACLETE PRESS
BREWSTER, MASSACHUSETTS

Everyday Catholic Prayer

2006 First Printing This Edition

Copyright © 1998, 1999, 2006 by Angela Tilby

ISBN: 1-55725-510-5

First published by
Arthur James Ltd.
70 Cross Oak Road
Berkhamsted
Hertfordshire HP4 3HZ Great Britain

Library of Congress Cataloging-in-Publication Data

Tilby, Angela.
  Everyday Catholic prayer : a little office book / Angela Tilby.
      p. cm.
  Includes bibliographical references and index.
  ISBN 1-55725-510-5 (hardcover : alk. paper)
  1. Catholic Church—Prayer-books and devotions—English. I. Title.
  BX2130.T55 2006
  242'.802—dc22

                          2006015950

10 9 8 7 6 5 4 3 2 1

Published by Paraclete Press
Brewster, Massachusetts
www.paracletepress.com

Printed in the United States of America

CONTENTS

INTRODUCTION

THE HABIT OF PRAYER

*T*his prayer book is designed for people who are looking for a simple and adaptable form of daily prayer. It is meant to be said by people who usually pray alone and yet like to feel that they are tapping into the prayer of the wider community of the Church.

I designed it for my own use during the early 1980s. It lived in my daily planner between the calendar and the address book. I hoped, by compiling this office, to find a way of locating my daily life and work within the great sacrifice which, the Church teaches, Christ offered to the Father on the cross, and which is recalled and reenacted at the Eucharist. I was trying to discover if prayer could bridge two worlds: the world of faith, on the one hand, and the secular, apparently godless world on the other. During the period in which the office was composed I was aware of a painful dissonance between these two ends of my experience. I could not understand how my working life could relate to what happened at the altar.

I think many of us find ourselves in a state of dissonance. Priests, nuns, and other religious may feel they are not very good at prayer, but at least they live a life which is structured in such a way that prayer time is expected and actually makes sense. But for many of us who live and work anonymously in a relentless secular environment, this is not so. Our Christian identity is something that can get lost, swallowed up by the general expectation that Christianity is simply dying on us. R.S. Thomas writes,

> The last quarter of the moon
> of Jesus gives way
> to the dark; the serpent
> digests the egg. . . .

> . . . Religion is over, and
> what will emerge from the body
> of the new moon, no one
> can say.

At such a time of uncertainty, prayer seems to be something we almost dare not attempt. Our "godless" humanity is all too apparent to us, all the time. We are suspicious of churches and creeds and holy books. But our doubts have not brought new insights. We are driven back on our private and personal lives, which now carry a weight of expectation and unsatisfied longing that they were perhaps never meant to bear. If we are created to find our rest in God alone, then the hunger for God will not go away when we cease to believe and practice faith. It will simply seek out a new focus. We deify work or success or pleasure or particular individuals.

Even among believers, prayer often seems a distracting luxury when children need taking to school or there's a pile of mail to be answered, or we're waiting anxiously for a phone call, or we don't know how the bills are going to be paid. We so easily feel judged, excluded by the failure to live up to what we think we should be. We would rather forget that we are Christians when our language and mood are foul, when we're behaving badly with our families, or we are being bullied at work. It seems almost dishonest to call upon God, to use words and phrases which the saints have used about our own often confusing or less than inspiring lives.

My question, when I began working with this prayer book, was whether I could find a way of being that confused and uninspired self in the presence of God. Could the dissonance between belief and life lead me to a new integrity? I found that when I was most aware of dissonance there were particular phrases from the Bible that came into my mind. One of the most persistent was, "I have labored in vain. I have spent my strength for nothing and vanity," words from Isaiah 49, one of the so-called Servant Songs of Second Isaiah. It summed up a sense of frustration and inadequacy. I found myself wondering whether I could link my personal response to those words to some universal meaning. The Servant Songs were to be one of the pivots of the office.

For a time I called the prayer book "The Office of the Servant." This was partly because of the Isaiah passages, but also because there was also a lot of interest at the time in the role of deacons. The word "deacon" comes straight from the Greek *"diakonos,"* which means "servant." I had always had difficulties with the concept of service. Although I had been brought up in a school environment where "service" to society was an ideal, it was one I found mildly oppressive. The word itself sounded demeaning, humiliating. Milton's Lucifer, who lost his place in heaven because he said, "I will not serve," was a character I had some sympathy with. I was also aware of a kind of rhetoric of service that is often applied to women, particularly in the churches. I was sensitive to the way in which women are often welcomed in subordinate, supportive roles, but have a much harder time as leaders. Given all this I could not understand what it was about the Servant theme which drew me, but it continued to do so.

There was another surprise too. I had always thought of myself as more of a "God-centered" believer than a "Christ-centered" one. Yet as I went on working at the structure of this office I found I was drawn to the Christ-centered themes of incarnation, cross, and resurrection. It was as though I was held between opposites. The Christ-story was the counter-story to the life I felt I was actually living. At the time I was working in the glamourous and self-promoting world of television documentaries. So much of Christ's ministry was silent, patient, enclosed in a pattern of prayer and withdrawal. It was from this silence that he was able to engage, to preach the kingdom and heal, to accept rejection and failure as well as success and adulation. I wondered if I would ever be able to find a pattern which led me closer to equanimity.

People need forms of prayer which can be used at any time and in any place with the minimum of books and fuss, and which also make sense of the dilemmas of our world. What is important is to try to be faithful in the midst of frustration, to find the resources just to go on with a difficult and unfulfilling task, to deal with one's own anxiety and frequent loss of courage. Doubt and difficulty can be plowed into the prayer and become part of what is offered.

I once spent a few days with the Sisters of the Love of God at Fairacres in Oxford. Their chapel is an Anglican version of an old-style Roman Catholic convent church. Their community literature and tradition places great importance on the sacrifice of

Christ, and the self-offering that is at the heart of their hidden contemplative life. They believe that, as Christ offers himself to the Father, so their offering of themselves is included and enclosed, its human failures made strong by his strength.

I thought of that band of women gathered in chapel for the cycle of the Daily Office. They had "put on the habit"—in their case, a chocolate-brown habit with a black veil. Together they seemed formidable in their anonymity. Yet I knew they were a strange mix of intelligence, eccentricity, wisdom, and fragility. Consecrated women as they were, they had their corporate and personal traumas just like everyone else. Was it hypocritical of them to devote themselves to prayer, to "wear" the habit of their profession? Or was part of what they brought to prayer the same ghastly mistakes, vanities, and stupidities that belong to all of us?

Many people never really get started on prayer because they feel they are not good enough for God to pay any attention to. Sometimes they suffer from childhood hurts that have never been healed; sometimes they are poor or ill-educated, or chronically ill; often they have been shamed by the loss of work, a damaging addiction, or the breakdown of a relationship. The Church seems to them to be for people who don't have these problems. They are wrong, of course. Church people have all these problems, but I wonder how often any of us hear the message that it is precisely *because* we are humiliated, weak, and nervous that God calls us into his company? The misery is often where we start from. The ingredients of despair are sometimes all we have to offer. As I prayed the Office I began to see that the meaning of Christ was a great exchange between humanity and God. The weak and fitful desire that I brought to prayer could be plunged into the immortal fire of Christ's self-sacrifice.

The clue to what was going on seemed to me to have something to do with *kenosis*, the renunciation of the divine nature, at least in part, by Christ in the incarnation. The word comes from the Greek word for "empty": the "self-emptying" of God is implied by the incarnation, and is spelled out in St. Paul's famous meditation on the humility of Christ in Philippians 2. *Kenosis* is the pattern by which God relates to us. There is a humiliation in God's coming to share our condition in Christ, and an exaltation, by which Christ is raised to glory, taking us with him. There is a vertical movement from glory to humility and back to glory.

By way of contrast, in the pattern of my own life there seemed to be a horizontal movement, from belief to unbelief and back again. I wanted to see whether the two movements could be related, to discover whether I could make sense of the dissonance between my two worlds by reflecting on the "distance" that the Son of God travels in coming to share our nature. And by reflecting on what it means to be offered in Christ, to be accepted within his sacrifice.

> Look, Father, look on his anointed face
> And only look on us as found in him. . . .

Perhaps praying was a way of "putting on a habit," "putting on Christ." This is difficult because we live in an age which believes in the absolute validity of personal self-expression. Emotional sincerity is a primary virtue. Acknowledging a gap between our ideals and our actual behavior is a vice, condemned as "hypocrisy." This is why people think that churchgoers must be hypocrites. They are pretending to be good, but everyone knows they cannot be really. To *not* go to church is at least to be honest and sincere, better than those hypocrites who go.

I was aware of this attitude as my own when I wanted to take up active Christian faith as a teenager. It seemed to me then that any "gap" in my believing or in behavior invalidated my commitment. If I wasn't being a perfect Christian I couldn't be one at all. There *had* to be identity between my inner experience and my outer self.

This relentless requirement that we be all of a piece is heightened in a media age. The media jump on "hypocrisy" because our fear of gaps and holes in the moral structure of the self is so enormous that we cannot endure it in others. No one can afford to have a private life unless it is the mirror image of their public life. We insist on "transparency" even while we find ourselves opaque.

I find this obsession with "hypocrisy" puzzling. Jesus condemned people as "hypocrites" when they had no access to their inner lives and sense of sin and weakness. We on the other hand admire precisely those who appear to be shiny bright all the way through. What Jesus saw as hypocritical we applaud as sincere. Yet when a public figure acknowledges a gap between his public and private selves we are ready to brand him as a hypocritical liar. What has happened to our capacity for moral discernment?

I think what is happening is that as Christianity is becoming less available as a normal way of life, we are becoming vulnerable to all kinds of pagan concepts of the self and God. Some of these have value and should not always be dismissed, but one which I think can be pernicious is the notion that the true self is a kind of *naked* self, a transparent self with no secrets. The true self is the one that talks about itself, that is cleansed by open confession. Reparation is not necessary because the very act of speaking frankly restores transparency and gives others grounds for confidence. The true self is realized in this life, not by *practicing* faith, patience, or courage, but simply by self-exposure. To practice a virtue brings a note of artificiality into the process, a touch of "hypocrisy." We are all being turned relentlessly into emotional flashers.

Yet although our society appears to believe in the value of the spontaneous self, it only half believes that the true self is a good self. Transparency is actually very threatening to most of us, precisely because we do have an inner life which needs its own space and privacy in which to grow. This may or may not be full of dark secrets, but it is ours, and it is often a yearning from this inner self which leads us to long to be able to pray. Our society denies the validity of the inner self and so it will always label prayer as hypocritical.

Spirituality, on the other hand, has become something of an "in" word. It is cool, it is a skill, a technique of self-improvement. And that brings us to the paradox which is inherent in our desire for naturalness. We are afflicted by the pressure of an endless demand for endless self-improvement. So, the pure body is not only a naked body, but a *trained* body, muscular and male, even for women, hard, free of softness and fat. The trained body can be shown off. It is a window to the soul. The physical and mental discipline displayed by the smooth lines announce that we are integrated through and through. The trained body is a guarantee that we are pure, sincere, straightforward, transparent selves. What you see is what you get. No lumps or bumps or unexpected crevices.

This idealization of the body has come to us through the culture of ancient Greece. The Greeks celebrated the male human form in sculpture, making images more perfect than any real body could ever be. The illusion of this trained nudity is that bodily perfection is somehow natural. Of course it is anything but natural. Thin bodies and muscular limbs are a highly artificial creation determined by our cultural preferences. Habit, discipline, and training are certainly relevant to Christian discipleship, and St. Paul uses an athletic contest as a metaphor for Christian perseverance.

But on the whole Christianity uses a rather different set of traditions in its depiction of the self. These come from the Hebrew Bible. The ancient Hebrews were uncomfortable with nudity. They seem to have experienced nakedness as a kind of shamefulness, of being less than human, rather than most fully human. Adam's recognition of his nakedness in the Garden of Eden is a moment of humiliation. His instinct is to cover himself. To be human is not to be naked but to be clothed, and God in his mercy clothes Adam and Eve in fur skins to cover their vulnerability. We need to have something added to us in order to be ourselves.

The metaphor of clothing has different consequences from the metaphor of nakedness. In the Greek view it is by taking away or removing our clothing, habits, surplus flesh, that we become natural and so fulfilled. In biblical and Christian language it is by being clothed and covered that we become the selves we are destined to become. What is natural is weak and unformed; nature needs to be fired by spirit.

The usual "habit" of Christian prayer is a habit that assumes we need to have something added to us rather than taken away. St. Paul's writings are full of metaphors of clothing. We are to "put on the armor of light" (Romans 13:12). In the resurrection the mortal will put on immortality (1 Corinthians 15:54). "Put on the Lord Jesus Christ," Paul says, "and make no provision for the lusts of the flesh." "While we are still in this (earthly) tent, we sigh with anxiety; not that we would be unclothed, but that we would be further clothed, so that what is mortal may be swallowed up by life" (2 Corinthians 5:4). What is the "clothing" that is added to us through the acceptance of Christian faith? What is the habit that we have to learn to wear?

It is surely the story of Christ, the pattern of Christ, the clothing of Christ, which is the template in which our own story, pattern, habit is to grow to maturity. To a "Greek" mindset this may look like a form of hypocrisy. Who am I to "put on" Christ? Shall I lose my authenticity, my "nakedness," my transparency and spontaneity, that of myself which is unique and which I value?

The experience of struggling with prayer at a time like ours is that these questions are put to us and will accompany us. We need such questions to provoke and inspire, but I believe that in experience they are actually transcended without ever being answered directly. The mystery is to find that our story is also Christ's story. It is naked that we come to Christ and helpless that we look to him for dress. So to pray the prayer of Christ is to move between weakness and power, vulnerability and strength. What began in painful dissonance continues as a purposeful cycle in which we are made aware of our vulnerability as we are given a secure identity in Christ.

WHAT IS AN OFFICE?

"OFFICE" is anglicized from the Latin word *officium*, which means a dutiful or respectful action. The offices of the Church are the obligatory prayers said by priests, monks, and nuns, usually at set times of day and night. Sometimes they are joined by lay volunteers. Traditionally, the regular offices are Morning and Evening Prayer. If you are an enclosed contemplative there may be seven daily offices of which Lauds and Vespers are the two most important. Some groups of Christians add to a morning and evening office a brief form of common mid-day prayer and Compline, bedtime prayer.

The idea of girding the twenty-four-hour cycle of the day with structured regular prayer has Jewish origins. There is a reference in the 119th Psalm to praising God seven times a day, and Psalm 134 calls on the servants of the Lord to stand before him in the temple at night. Early Christian worship stemmed from Jewish liturgy. It developed as a pattern of psalms, readings, and prayers, all based on the Scriptures.

The basic elements of an office are psalms, readings from Scripture, canticles, and prayers. Often there is also a hymn and a responsive form of prayer. To take part in an office is like taking part in a conversation with the Word of God. You listen to the Word, and you respond with the Word. But paradoxically, though the words of Scripture and psalmody are the building blocks of the office, they are also a vehicle for contemplation which passes beyond words. The words are taken up by the Word. The Word moves us to silence.

Alongside the formal office of the Church there has been a tendency to make simpler versions for those whose commitments did not permit them to participate in the whole thing. There is, for example, a Little Office of Our Lady which came into use in the tenth century. It is shaped like the Divine Office, but is much shorter, and uses the same psalms each day. It became particularly popular among laypeople, who could say it while about their other tasks. Although not an office as such, the Rosary performs a similar function, as does the Jesus Prayer. These forms of prayer are based on limited, repeated material—in the case of the Jesus Prayer this is a single sentence! These forms of prayer don't take long to say and they don't require extra books or lectionaries. This is the tradition that this Little Office is seeking to follow.

THE STRUCTURE OF
EVERYDAY CATHOLIC PRAYER

Invocation

"O come. . . ." These words come from the daily prayer used by Eastern Orthodox Christians. They echo the psalms of invitation, like Psalm 95, the *Venite*, which begins with the words, "O come, let us sing to the Lord . . .," and is often used at the beginning of worship. Here, the focus of worship is Christ the Lord. We do not worship God in the abstract or in theory, but as he is in his personal relationship with us.

The Office begins with a call to worship that is both solemn and celebratory. When you say this alone, the words "O come . . ." are an invitation to gather oneself together, joining the communion of saints in earth and heaven in the worship of God revealed in Christ.

"Jesus Christ, the Alpha and the Omega. . . ." These words are adapted from the opening prayers of the Easter liturgy.

Refrains on the Psalms

Because the set psalms are the same every day, the refrains are used at the beginning and end to give a particular color to each day of the week. All the refrains are phrases taken from other psalms. The psalms are set out with a colon in the middle of each verse. This is because one meditative way of saying the psalms is to make a brief pause at the colon. This is particularly helpful in establishing a rhythm when a group is saying the psalms together, but it will slow you down and help you not to rush if you are saying them alone.

The Psalms

Christians have always used the Psalms of the Hebrew Scriptures as a treasury both of personal prayer and communal worship. The psalms have an extraordinary capacity for expressing feelings, whether of praise or pain. When they are used in a structured office like this, they have three levels of meaning.

First, they are simply marvelous prayers to God, expressing trust, thanksgiving, grief, and hope. They can be personal and universal at the same time.

Second, they unite us with the past. They link us to the worship of the ancient temple in Jerusalem and with the hopes of the Jewish people. The psalms were composed over five centuries. Some probably go back to the earliest days of King David's dynasty, others reflect the time after the exile.

They link us very directly with Jesus. As a Jew he would have known the psalms. He quoted them in his teaching, and, according to three of the Gospels, he was praying words from them when he died on the cross. The psalms also link us to the Church down through the ages, to monks and hermits, priests and scribes, matriarchs and patriarchs, saints and sinners.

Third, they are the prayer of Christ, praying through us and for us. The expressions of trust and fear, love and anxiety all belong to our human condition. It is this condition which the Son of God took on in the Incarnation and in which he suffered, died, and rose again. So praying the psalms is enclosing ourselves within the being of Christ, making his story our own, and our own, his.

The three psalms set here belong to a collection which is described as "songs of ascents." This means that they were probably originally sung as pilgrimage songs by Jews on the way up to Jerusalem for the great festivals of the Jewish year. They remind us that the drama of salvation was played out in Jerusalem. It was the city of the crucifixion and resurrection, of the humiliation and exaltation of Christ. They also remind us of our own life's journey. We move daily towards the city of engagement with others and the tasks we have to fulfill, and at the same time towards the heavenly city of fulfillment.

PSALM 121
"I lift up my eyes to the hills. . . ."

This is a psalm of confidence in God. The word translated as "keeper" has the sense of guardian, watchman, and protector, and it is repeated over again to give it mounting force. It's easy to imagine bands of weary pilgrims straining for the first sight of Jerusalem through the hills of Judea. On the long, steep climb they would have needed protection from the blazing sun. Sunstroke was a real danger. The pilgrims would have shared with other ancient peoples the fear of the bad influence of the moon. The goal of their journey was the temple, and the temple was God's dwelling place, the Holy of Holies, a totally empty space without any kind of image. It was in this emptiness that the pilgrims placed their confidence. The Jews have always known that though God chooses to dwell with his people, he does not occupy space. His being is eternal mystery. He is both beyond and above all that we can know of him.

In the Christian era this psalm is often used at times of transition. It is appropriate for both marriages and funerals because it stresses God's constant, watchful protection over us. He is an "unsleeping Lord." Though our circumstances change, he is constant. In the heat of our engagement with the stresses and conflicts of life, he is cool shadow. In our beginnings, and in our dyings and grievings, in the chill of anxiety and at the birth of hope, he is safety. He gives us the space to go in and out, to become involved and committed to the tasks of life and to withdraw in peace. Our confidence is well-founded because God is the maker of heaven and earth, holding all creation and all our destinies in his hands.

Reading the psalm as the prayer of Christ reminds us that the goal of Christ's pilgrimage on earth is to bring us, with him, to the Father. His gaze is focused on God. The source of his being is above and beyond this world. The Gospels show us how his mission leads him inexorably, step by step, towards Jerusalem. There is no escaping this destiny: "He will not let your foot be moved. . . ." The city is the scene of his greatest conflict and triumph. Our way to the Father means treading in the footsteps of Christ.

PSALM 124
*"If it had not been
the Lord who was on our side. . . ."*

This is a psalm of thanksgiving. It was probably used at times of deliverance from political or military danger. The use of "Israel" suggests that it could have been a kind of national hymn. The threat is described in two ways. It is first a threat of being engulfed and swallowed up, with the loss of identity that such disaster entails. It is also the threat of being hunted down by lions or wolves, or being trapped like a bird. Floods are a frequent Biblical symbol of chaos and terror. They evoke the unformed "waste and void" before the act of creation, and the ever-present reality of Sheol, the shadowy realm of the dead in which "all things are forgotten."

In a Christian context this is a psalm thanking God for salvation especially at times of persecution. In the early centuries of Christianity believers really did face lions and wolves, and the only salvation they could hope for was beyond this world. The mood of thanksgiving for deliverance is important in the Christian pilgrimage. It is often by remembering and recounting the ways in which God has stood by us in the past that we gain confidence for the future. As in the earlier psalm, it is because God holds the world in his hands that we can be sure of his help.

Reading the psalm as the prayer of Christ, we are reminded of the despair that overwhelmed Christ in Gethsemane and on the cross. It was for us that he faced the annihilation of hope. He identified with us so deeply that the early Christian writers can say he descended into hell. Yet he, like Israel, is vindicated by God. The deep waters of death do not hold him for ever; the snare of the tomb is broken and he rises from the dead to set us free.

PSALM 126

"When the Lord restored the fortunes of Zion. . . ."

This is a psalm of lament, pleading with God to act for his people as he has done in the past. Older translations appear to contain a reference to Israel's exile and restoration, "When the Lord turned again the captivity of Zion . . .," but it makes better sense of the Hebrew to refer to the Lord restoring the fortunes of Zion. Some people think it was composed shortly after the Exile, when the enormity of the task of restoration became apparent. But others think it has no particular historical reference. The version here is an adaptation of existing versions. There is a pleading atmosphere to the psalm. God's earlier vindication of his people aroused admiration from the nations. The prayer for restoration is repeated. The rivers of the South are the water-courses of the arid land known as the Negev. The riverbeds are dried up by the summer drought, but they fill up and flow again with the autumn rains. The psalm looks forward to a fruitful outcome to the present suffering.

In a Christian context this is a psalm about the restoration of confidence in a time of dryness and unfruitfulness. There is a positive use of the imagination to steel our will to hope even when things seem barren. Dreams are not all negative fantasy, they are also places of revelation. At a time of the decline of committed faith we need to have a steady longing of what it would be like for some common Christian life to be restored. At times of personal grief we need a dream of wholeness. At the same time, we must not cut short the process of healing and renewal by what therapists call a premature "flight into health." It is a time to "take no thought of the harvest, but only of proper sowing," as the Rock says in T.S. Eliot's Choruses from *The Rock*. This means, in the first instance, acknowledging realistically the spiritual, emotional, and intellectual poverty that has us in its grip. The last two verses are hugely reassuring. What is undertaken at such times may have only our tears to water it, but, the promise is, the tears themselves can bring the seed to life and ensure a joyful harvest.

Reading this psalm as the prayer of Christ is to be drawn to his passion for the kingdom of God. In the parables the kingdom is often understood organically —the word is sown randomly in human hearts, and some human hearts bring forth fruit. The kingdom is like the seed that grows secretly and at night. It does not conform to predictable patterns of growth. The kingdom is also close to those who are broken and poor. There is no distinction between the sinners and the victims—all who are able to acknowledge their need of God are citizens of God's kingdom. The psalm also reminds us of the suffering and passion of Christ. When he reached Jerusalem after his last pilgrim journey, he wept over it. In John's Gospel he speaks of the seed that must fall into the ground and die in order to produce a harvest. The psalm brings us back to the central theme of the Office, the dying and rising of Christ, through which our own lives are transformed and renewed.

The Song of the Servant

These seven readings come from the middle section of the book of Isaiah, which was written during the Exile in Babylon, at the point where restoration was on the horizon. The prophet (we don't know his name, though his work is collected under the name of the earlier prophet Isaiah) is addressing a situation of despair and cynicism, tinged with nostalgia. The overwhelming theme of his prophecy is hope. The people are to stop wallowing in the past and prepare themselves for God's future. The future is not mapped out in any detail; the hardship and struggle of the real return are not even hinted at. The prophet's dream is of a triumphant march back to Zion, with nature itself obligingly helping by lowering mountains and raising valleys on the way. But that is not the whole of this prophet's message. He points to a figure called the servant of the Lord who is in some way the sign and key to what God is bringing about. The servant is never quite identified; sometimes he is called Israel, sometimes he is a strange, anonymous figure. In other passages in this text he is identified with Cyrus, who has just conquered Babylon and started a new dynasty. When he speaks of the servant in the first person the prophet may even be drawing on his own experience as a preacher to the exiles. The vocation of the servant is strangely described with mounting intensity as one who is called to suffering, frustration, and silence. Yet he bears his failure and indignity with patience, and in the end is rewarded by God.

Behold my servant . . .

The servant is called and chosen and he bears the Spirit of God. His vocation leads beyond Israel to the nations, yet his mission is carried out without speech. He does not judge his fellows. Though faith and strength are failing, he does not condemn or patronize, nor does he give up.

The Lord called me . . .

The servant speaks in this passage about his call in terms similar to that of the prophet Jeremiah. He has been given the sharp mouth of a prophet, but he is hidden away in God's hand. God names him as Israel in whom he will be glorified. But the note of frustration now creeps in. The servant has labored in vain; he has exhausted himself and seen no improvement. Yet he remains committed to God and to his cause. And God actually heightens the stakes, charging him with a mission not only to restore Israel but to bring light and salvation to the pagan world.

> *The Lord God has given me the tongue of those who are taught . . .*

The servant shares in the condition of the people; he speaks as one who is himself a learner. His vocation is bound up with listening; every morning he listens to God and he begins to hear as his people hear. Now the painful cost of his call becomes evident. He is under attack. He is spat at and shamed. He does not retaliate, nor does he give up. He sets his face like flint and endures, believing that God will stand by him in the end.

> *Behold, my servant shall prosper . . .*

This is the beginning of the passion narrative of the servant. He is to be lifted up, like a figure being enthroned, but what will people see? A shocking appearance that will stun the powerful into silence. A dialogue begins in the presence of this wounded figure. What does God mean by him?

> *He grew up before him . . .*

The servant is a figure with no advantages. He is a root from dry ground, unlikely to be fruitful. He has no natural attractiveness. He seems born to sorrow.

People turn away from him so as not to have to face him in his grief. At this point we begin to sense a sympathy for the servant, a recognition of likeness within unlikeness. Although he cannot be looked at there is the beginning of a recognition that the sorrow he carries is not only his own.

All we like sheep . . .

The story of the servant begins to evoke not only sympathy but repentance. His silence in the face of suffering moves those who watch. The passage hints at a lonely, disgraceful death without the vindication hinted at in the earlier passages. Yet there is also a recognition that this death is not an accident. It is intimately related to the condition of the people.

He shall see his offspring . . .

There will be a reversal, though the means are not described. The faithfulness of the servant will bring about the fruitful response he longed for. His life and death will have played their part in converting the people from despair to hope.

* * *

As with the psalms, we can take these readings on three levels. The servant passages are so familiar within a Christian context, especially the fifty-third chapter which provides the inspiration for so much of Handel's *Messiah*, that it is important to be refreshed by the insights that come from the original historical setting. The servant figure is genuinely mysterious. I think that the prophet is trying to tap into his people's feelings that they have been washed up on the shores of history, their identity lost and forgotten. They have buried this pain under a superficial indifference. They have come to believe that there is no point in hope. The prophet describes the call of the servant, and then depicts the pathetic sufferings he has to endure.

In the fifty-third chapter the prophet invites the people's pity and compassion. There is a dialogue about the fate of the servant in which the people finally conclude that the servant will and must be vindicated after all that he has been through. In this way the prophet helps his people to acknowledge the shameful tragedy of their own circumstances. Only when they have done this will they be able to desire a better future. Without such desire being aroused they are condemned to a sterile existence. It is a stroke of poetic genius, in a message which is so overwhelmingly hopeful, to plant at its core the dark figure of the patient victim.

The servant figure speaks to the sense that many people have of being adrift and alienated from their humanity. We live in an age when millions are in internal exile, suffering from a chronic lack of self-esteem. Perhaps somewhere in our experience there was once a sense of vocation, that we had a particular destiny that would make our lives worthwhile. But often this has been frustrated, sometimes by lack of opportunity or by adversity, or by our own recurrent sense of failure.

If this has been our experience then we can recognize the story of the servant as touching our own personal history. We, like the exiled Jews, are called into dialogue as the extent of human suffering is revealed. We are invited to wonder at the sheer scale of the servant's pain, and so to be moved to compassion. By doing so we may find compassion for ourselves. Not the self-indulgent, self-promoting pity which invites admiration and so avoids real distress, but the stark clarity of seeing ourselves through a parallel history, in a face and fate we do not immediately recognize as our own. Through such recognition our vision can widen outward to understanding and compassion for those whose poverty and deprivation is not inner and spiritual but outer and material. All of us are called, together, to a new world, a return from the exile which separates us, not only from ourselves, but from one another.

In a Christian setting the fate of the servant points to the life and self-offering of Christ. It touches our celebration of Christ's life at many points. The call of the servant is echoed in the Gospel stories of Jesus' baptism; the summons to be a "light to the nations" is taken up in Luke's Gospel in the Song of Simeon, the *Nunc Dimittis*.

Some commentators think that the description of the servant's trials may have actually influenced the way the Gospel writers describe the passion of Christ. His silence before his judges, his patient acceptance of shame and indignity, certainly seem to echo Isaiah's servant. His patient bearing of punishment for sin is expanded and reinterpreted in the writings of both St. John and St. Paul. His vindication is spelled out in the New Testament conviction of his resurrection and exaltation into heaven. From Advent to Pentecost, the story of the Servant is now deeply embedded in the mind of Christians. But the heart of it is the paschal mystery, Christ's descent into suffering and the eventual fruitfulness of his patience.

God the Holy . . .

These words are known as the Trisagion, the "three times holy." Another version is to say, "Holy God, Holy and strong, Holy and immortal, have mercy on us." The words are used in the liturgies of the Orthodox churches before the epistle and Gospel readings. In the Western Church the Trisagion is prayed on Good Friday.

Canticle Refrains

Like the refrains on the psalms, these short quotations from Scripture are intended to give a particular daily focus to the canticle.

Canticle of Christ's Glory

The word *canticle* comes from the Latin word for song, and is used for verses derived from Scripture that are used in the Church's worship. This canticle is an astonishing hymn to Christ which appears in St. Paul's letter to the Philippians. Whether Paul composed it himself or is quoting a devotional poem which already existed is not certain. What is certain is that it must have been the custom of the Church from very early times to worship Christ in hymns. This letter pre-dates any of the four Gospels. It is proof that Christianity was, in a sense, born in song. In AD 112 the governor of the Roman province of Bithynia wrote to the emperor Trajan for advice on handling the Christian community. He told him it was their custom to meet on the first day of the week and sing a hymn to Christ *"quasi Deo,"* as to a god.

The context of this particular hymn is advice that the apostle is delivering to the Philippian Christians. They are, he says, to "have this mind among your-selves which is yours in Christ Jesus, who, though he was in the form of God, did not count equality with God a thing to be grasped, but emptied himself, taking the form of a servant, and being born in the likeness of men." It is notoriously difficult to produce a good translation of these words in simple English, and my own is probably more simple than illuminating. But the general sense is clear enough: The coming of Christ into our world is an act of profound humility and identification with human beings, which should call forth from us humility towards God and identification with each other's needs. It both takes up the theme of the servant passages from Isaiah and moves beyond them.

Behind the hymn is the Jewish concept of the wisdom of God. Wisdom is the subject of many of the Proverbs, and of the Wisdom of Solomon and the book of Ecclesiasticus. These play on the idea of wisdom as a personification of God's creativity. Wisdom accompanies God in the making of the world. She is God's inspiration and delight. In the Wisdom of Solomon she is depicted as "a breath of the power of God, and a pure emanation of the glory of the Almighty . . . a reflection of eternal light, a spotless mirror of the working of God" (Wisdom 7:25-26). Wisdom is also described as "passing into holy souls, making them friends of God and prophets" (Wisdom 7:27b). In the Proverbs, Wisdom is sometimes portrayed as a merchant in the marketplace selling her wares, and inviting the wise and foolish to learn from her. The teachings of Jesus have something of the flavor of this Jewish wisdom about them. Jesus points to the difference between wisdom and folly in the parable of the houses built on rock and sand, and in the parable of the wise and foolish virgins. In the hymn of Philippians Jesus is worshiped as God's wisdom, who lays aside the life of glory he shares with God to enter our condition, binding himself to our fate even to the point of death. Because of this he is exalted and given the same royal name as God himself.

The Wisdom of Jesus

These seven short Gospel readings have been chosen to illustrate the theme of humiliation and exaltation within the teaching of Jesus. When the Gospel book is brought in surrounded by candles during the Eastern Orthodox liturgy the priest intones, "Wisdom, stand up!" The entrance of the Gospel recalls Jesus as the light of the world and as God's wisdom. The translation used here is the New Revised Standard Version.

If anyone would come after me . . .

This word of Jesus appears in the Gospels of Mark, Matthew, and Luke. All three books place it after the dialogue Jesus has with his disciples in which Peter grasps the truth of his identity. He is "the Christ of God." Immediately Jesus spells out what it means to be a follower of God's Christ. Clinging to proud or anxious self-definitions and self-advertisements is the sure way to lose who we really are. Taking up the cross is the mark of discipleship. Luke alone points out that this is a daily task, a task renewed on the first day of the working week.

Come to me, you that labor . . .

This word of Jesus is unique to Matthew. Jesus speaks here as the embodiment of Wisdom who lays out her stall in the marketplace of life, and makes her offer of life to the wise and foolish alike. Jesus addresses himself particularly to the burdened, the poor, the overworked, and the worried, to all who say to themselves, "I have labored in vain." These are the people who are "yoked," burdened by the obligation of having to carry heavy loads for others. In the Hebrew Scriptures, freedom is often described as having a yoke broken. Jesus uses the metaphor of the yoke to describe the paradox that his service is freedom; the yoke he offers is gentler than the mere absence of constraint.

You know that among the Gentiles . . .

The world Jesus lived in was dominated by the Roman Empire. The social structure he would have associated with Gentiles was a pyramid. At the top were a very few, who had control over the lives of the masses. Jesus suggests that such structures are bound to be crippling; they cannot express the life of the kingdom. Among disciples there is to be a structure of service rather than control. Ambition is not negated, but it must go by the route of humility. This is what it means to follow the Son of Man, whose life is paid out to set many free.

The kingdom of God is as if . . .

This word of Jesus is unique to Mark. It is a parable of the kingdom which suggests that its coming is both hidden and inevitable. We are not in control of the processes which bring it. This should bring us relief; we are not to live from guilt, but from grace. What we are responsible for is sowing and reaping; committing ourselves to the life and the tasks we have been given and discerning the moment at which our commitment demands decisive action.

The hour has come . . .

Jesus says these words in response to a request from some Greeks—non-Jews—who wish to see him. What is spelled out is the cost of "seeing him" as he is, which is no less than death and resurrection. This is spelled out on three levels. It is a simple truth of nature that, for a seed to produce fruit, it must cease to be a seed. The "single grain" must die to create a harvest. In the same way the Son of Man, as the embodiment of the call of Israel, must die for the divine life to become available to the world. The glory can only come through the agony of the cross. The same pattern is lived by Jesus' followers. We must live lightly to the life of this world if we are to be transparent to the life of eternity. This saying is chosen for Fridays because Friday is traditionally a day to remember the death of Jesus on the cross.

What woman, having ten silver coins . . .

This parable is unique to Luke. Like the parable of the lost sheep which precedes it, this is a story illustrating God's watchful and searching care for individuals. To consider a person as lost is to indicate how precious they are. God's concern for his lost children is likened to that of a woman who turns her house upside down to find what is most valuable to her. The point is that God is just as concerned as we would be in searching for what is lost and just as happy when he finds it. This story is chosen for Saturdays because this is often a day for domesticity, when our true values are revealed and lived.

Let anyone who is thirsty . . .

Sunday is the day of refreshment, when we are fed by the Word of God in Scripture and sacrament. This word of Jesus is set "on the last day of the feast, the great day," which was probably a Sabbath. The feast referred to was the Feast of Tabernacles, when Jews remind themselves of their total dependence on God during the wandering in the wilderness. Water is a necessity for life, but here Jesus says that there is a thirst which is more than physical, which he can quench in his own person. Those who drink from the well that Jesus offers, themselves become conduits of God's life-bearing Spirit.

HOW TO SAY THE LITTLE OFFICE

Everyday Catholic Prayer takes about five minutes to say. Before you begin, try to quiet your mind and body. Some people find deep breathing helps. Try to withdraw consciously into a place of emptiness and peace. If you are alone and are not used to using set forms of prayer, it may help to say the words aloud. If you are in a quiet place you might want to cross yourself as you begin to say the Office or to light a candle beforehand. The refrains on the psalms and canticle can be said several times, if you wish, before and after the psalms and canticle. Remember that though you are alone, you are using words from Scripture and tradition which millions of believers have treasured. On the blank pages, you may wish to add your own prayers. Remember that to pray is to join worshipers from all over the world, and from all times and ages.

THE OFFICE

INVOCATION

O come, let us worship
God our King.

O come, let us worship
and fall down before Christ
our King and our God.

O come, let us worship
and fall down before Christ himself,
our King and our God.

Jesus Christ, the Alpha and the Omega!
He is the same yesterday, today and for ever;
come, let us worship.

REFRAINS ON THE PSALMS

These may be said at the beginning and end of each psalm.

Monday
My times, Lord, are in your hand:
When I wake I am still with you.

Tuesday
With you is the well of life:
And in your light do we see light.

Wednesday
My tongue is the pen of a ready writer:
I address my verses to the King.

Thursday
The Lord is my shepherd:
Therefore I can lack nothing.

Friday
The angel of the Lord encamps:
Around those who fear him.

Saturday
The Lord is my light and my salvation:
Whom shall I fear?

Sunday
You have said, "Seek my face":
Your face, Lord, do I seek.

PSALMS

PSALM 121

I lift up my eyes to the hills: from where is my help to come?

My help comes from the Lord: the maker of heaven and earth.

He will not let your foot be moved: and he who watches over you will not fall asleep.

Behold, he who keeps watch over Israel: shall neither slumber nor sleep;

The Lord himself watches over you: the Lord is your shade at your right hand,

So that the sun shall not strike you by day: nor the moon by night.

The Lord shall preserve you from all evil: it is he who shall keep you safe.

The Lord shall watch over your going out and your coming in: from this time forth forevermore.

PSALM 124

If the Lord had not been on our side: let Israel now say;

If the Lord had not been on our side: when enemies rose up against us;

Then would they have swallowed us up alive: in their fierce anger towards us;

Then would the waters have overwhelmed us: and the torrent gone over us;

Then would the raging waters: have gone right over us;

Blessed be the Lord: he has not given us over to be a prey for their teeth.

We have escaped like a bird from the snare of the fowler: the snare is broken and we have escaped.

Our help is in the name of the Lord: the maker of heaven and earth.

PSALM 126

When the Lord restored the fortunes of Zion: we were like those who dream.

Then our mouth was filled with laughter: and our tongue with shouts of joy.

Then they said among the nations: "The Lord has done great things for them."

Yea, the Lord has done great things for us: and we are glad indeed.

Restore our fortunes, O Lord: as the rivers in the south.

Those who sowed with tears: will reap with songs of joy.

Those who go out weeping, carrying the seed: will come again with joy, shouldering their sheaves.

THE SONG OF THE SERVANT

Monday

Behold my servant whom I uphold, my chosen, in whom my soul delights. I have put my Spirit upon him, he will bring forth justice to the nations. He will not cry or lift up his voice, or make it heard in the street. A bruised reed he will not break and a failing flax he will not quench. He will faithfully bring forth justice. He will not fail or be discouraged until he has established justice in the earth, and the coastlands wait for his law.   *Isaiah 42:1–4*

Tuesday

The Lord called me from the womb, from the body of my mother he named my name. He made my mouth like a sharp sword, in the shadow of his hand he hid me away. And he said to me, You are my servant Israel, in whom I will be glorified. But I said, I have labored in vain. I have spent my strength for nothing and vanity. Yet surely my right is with the Lord and my recompense with my God.

And now the Lord says, who formed me from the womb to be his servant, to bring back Jacob to him, for I am honored in the eyes of the Lord, and my God has become my strength—he says, "It is too light a thing that you should be my servant to raise up the tribes of Jacob and to restore the preserved of

Israel; I will give you as a light to the nations, that my salvation may reach to the ends of the earth."

Isaiah 49:1–5

Wednesday

The Lord God has given me the tongue of those who are taught, that I may know how to sustain with a word him that is weary. Morning by morning he wakens, he wakens my ear to hear as those who are taught. The Lord God opened my ear and I was not rebellious. I gave my back to the smiters and my cheeks to those who pulled out my beard. I hid not my face from shame and spitting.

For the Lord God helps me. Therefore I have set my face like flint, and I know that I shall not be put to shame: he who vindicates me is near.

Isaiah 50:4–8a

Thursday

Behold my servant shall prosper, he shall be exalted and lifted up, and shall be very high. As many were astonished at him—his appearance was so marred beyond human semblance, and his form beyond that of the sons of men—so shall he startle many nations; kings shall shut their mouths because of him; for that which has not been told them they shall see, and that which they have not heard they shall understand.

Who has believed our report? And to whom has the arm of the Lord been revealed?

Isaiah 52:13–53:1

Friday

He grew up before him like a young plant, and like a root out of dry ground; he had no form or comeliness that we should look at him, and no beauty that we should desire him. He was despised and rejected by men, a man of sorrows and acquainted with grief; and as one from whom men hide their faces, he was despised and we esteemed him not.

Surely he has borne our griefs and carried our sorrows; yet we esteemed him stricken, smitten by God and afflicted. But he was wounded for our transgressions, he was bruised for our iniquities; upon him was the chastisement that made us whole, and with his stripes we are healed. *Isaiah 53:2–5*

Saturday

All we like sheep have gone astray; we have turned everyone to his own way; and the Lord has laid on him the iniquity of us all.

He was oppressed and he was afflicted, yet he opened not his mouth; like a lamb that is led to the slaughter, and like a sheep that before its shearers is dumb, he opened not his mouth. By oppression and judgment he was taken away, and as for his generation, who considered that he was cut off from the land of the living, stricken for the transgression of my people? And they made his grave with the wicked, and with a rich man in his death, although he had done no violence, and there was no deceit in his mouth. *Isaiah 53:6–9*

Sunday

It was the will of the Lord to bruise him; he has put him to grief; when he makes himself an offering for sin, he shall see his offspring, he shall prolong his days. The will of the Lord shall prosper in his hand; he shall see the fruit of the travail of his soul and be satisfied. By his knowledge shall the righteous one, my servant, make many to be accounted righteous, and he shall bear their iniquities.

Therefore I will appoint him a portion with the great, and he shall divide the spoil with the strong, because he poured out his soul to death and was numbered with the transgressors; yet he bore the sin of many and made intercession for the transgressors.
Isaiah 53:10–12

This response may be said at the end of the reading:

God the Holy,
God the Strong,
God the Immortal One,
Have mercy on me.

CANTICLE REFRAINS

Monday
Revive your work, Lord, in the midst of the years.

Tuesday
Not by might, nor by power, but by my Spirit,
says the Lord.

Wednesday
What is sown is perishable,
what is raised is imperishable.

Thursday
Ask and it shall be given unto you, seek and you
shall find, knock and it shall be opened to you.

Friday
The Sun of righteousness shall rise
with healing in his wings.

Saturday
Blessed are those who have not seen,
and yet have believed.

Sunday
Christ in you, the hope of glory.

CANTICLE OF CHRIST'S GLORY

Christ Jesus was divine in form,
yet to God's form he did not cling:
    but emptied his immortal self,
    and took instead a servant's form.

In human likeness he was born,
in human form he found himself
    and humbled, he obeyed to death,
    death on a cross.

Therefore God raised him to the heights,
and gave to him the Name of names:
    that at the name of Jesus Christ
    all knees should bow and tongues confess
    that Jesus Christ is Lord,
    to God the Father's glory.

Glory be to the Father, and to the Son,
and to the Holy Spirit:
    as it was in the beginning,
    is now and ever shall be,
    world without end. Amen.

Philippians 2

Monday

If any want to become my followers, let them deny themselves and take up their cross daily and follow me. For those who want to save their life will lose it, and those who lose their life for my sake will save it. What does it profit them if they gain the whole world, but lose or forfeit themselves?   *Luke 9:23–25*

Tuesday

Come to me, all you who are weary and are carrying heavy burdens, and I will give you rest. Take my yoke upon you and learn from me; for I am gentle and humble in heart, and you will find rest for your souls. For my yoke is easy and my burden is light.

Matthew 11:28–30

Wednesday

You know that among the Gentiles those whom they recognize as their rulers lord it over them, and their great ones are tyrants over them. But it is not so among you; but whoever wishes to become great among you must be your servant, and whoever wishes to be first among you must be slave of all. For the Son of Man came not to be served but to serve and to give his life as a ransom for many.

Mark 10:42–45

Thursday

The kingdom of God is as if someone would scatter seed on the ground, and would sleep and rise night and day, and the seed would sprout and grow, he does not know how. The earth produces of itself, first the stalk, then the ear, then the full grain in the ear. But when the grain is ripe, at once he goes in with the sickle, because the harvest has come.

Mark 4:26–29

Friday

The hour has come for the Son of Man to be glorified. Very truly I tell you, unless a grain of wheat falls into the earth and dies, it remains just a single grain; but if it dies, it bears much fruit. Those who love their life lose it, and those who hate their life in this world will keep it for eternal life. Whoever serves me must follow me; and where I am, there will my servant be also.

John 12:23–26a

Saturday

What woman having ten silver coins, if she loses one of them, does not light a lamp, sweep the house, and search carefully until she finds it? When she has found it, she calls together her friends and neighbors, saying, "Rejoice with me, for I have found the coin that I had lost." Just so, I tell you, there is joy in the

presence of the angels of God over one sinner who
repents. *Luke 15:8–10*

Sunday

Let anyone who is thirsty come to me, and let the
one who believes in me drink. As the scripture has
said, "Out of the believer's heart shall flow rivers of
living water." Now he said this about the Spirit,
which believers in him were to receive.

John 7:37b–39a

This may be said after the reading:

Lord, have mercy upon us,
Christ, have mercy upon us,
Lord, have mercy upon us.

COLLECTS

These traditional prayers draw together the daily themes.

Monday

O God, by whose command the order of time runs its course: forgive our restlessness, perfect our faith, and, while we await the fulfillment of your promise, grant us to have a good hope through the Word made flesh, Jesus Christ our Lord. Amen.

Tuesday

Almighty God, you have made us for yourself and our hearts are restless until they find their rest in you: teach us to offer ourselves to your service, that here we may have your peace, and in the world to come may see you face to face; through Jesus Christ our Lord. Amen.

Wednesday

Eternal God and Father, by whose power we are created and by whose love we are redeemed: guide and strengthen us by your Spirit, that we may give ourselves in love and service to one another and to you, through our Lord Jesus Christ. Amen.

Thursday

Almighty God, in Christ you make all things new: transform the poverty of our nature by the riches of your grace, and in the renewal of our lives make known your heavenly glory; through Jesus Christ our Lord. Amen.

Friday

Lord God, whose blessed Son our Savior gave his back to the smiters and did not hide his face from shame: give us grace to endure the sufferings of this present time with sure confidence in the glory that shall be revealed; through Jesus Christ our Lord. Amen.

Saturday

O God, the protector of all who put their trust in you, without whom nothing is strong, nothing is holy: increase and multiply upon us your mercy that, you being our ruler and guide, we may so pass through things temporal that we finally lose not the things eternal; grant this, heavenly Father, for the sake of Jesus Christ our Lord. Amen.

Sunday

Lord our God, grant us grace to desire you with our whole heart: that so desiring, we may seek and find you; and so finding, may love you; and so loving, may hate those sins from which you have delivered us, through Jesus Christ our Lord. Amen.

THE LORD'S PRAYER

Our Father, who art in heaven,
Hallowed be thy name.
Thy kingdom come,
Thy will be done,
On earth as it is in heaven.
Give us this day our daily bread,
And forgive us our trespasses,
As we forgive those who trespass against us.
And lead us not into temptation,
But deliver us from evil,
For thine is the kingdom,
The power and the glory,
Forever and ever. Amen.

Conclusion

Let us bless the Lord.
Thanks be to God.

ADDITIONAL MATERIAL

EXPLANATORY·NOTE

Everyday Catholic Prayer is deliberately brief. To amplify it I have compiled this additional material as a collection of prayers and praises so that the book can be used more generally as a spiritual resource. You will find first a selection of canticles for morning and evening. These are the canticles used at Morning and Evening Prayer. You may wish to add them to the Little Office, or to say them independently. If you want to use them with the Office, the *Venite* and *Jubilate* should be used after the Invocation and before the psalms. The *Te Deum* and the *Benedicite* could be used at the end of the Office as a hymn of praise. The *Benedictus*, *Magnificat*, and *Nunc Dimittis* could either replace the Canticle of Christ's Glory, or be used after the short Gospel reading from the Wisdom of Jesus and before the Collect. You might want to add a period of intercession or silence before the Collect as well.

The other canticles may also be said as desired after the Invocation and before the psalms.

The prayers and meditations which follow can be used either before or after the Office or at any time.

A wide selection of psalms is included. This may seem odd. Why so many psalms when the readings set from the rest of Scripture for use with this office are so restricted? The reason is that the psalms hold a special place in Christian prayer, because, unlike other Scriptures, they are addressed directly to God. They are not primarily set out as narratives, as are the Old Testament histories, the Gospels, and the Acts. Nor are they primarily intended to teach or admonish or prophesy. No, their purpose is to engage with God directly as the intimate "thou" of our existence. It has often been said that the psalms encompass the whole range of human emotions. It is certainly true that as we pray them we shall find ourselves caught up in moods of gratitude, joy, praise; anxiety, horror, and grief. Nothing is left out. The psalms have provided the bedrock of the Church's corporate prayer since the early days of the monastic movement, and they still play a major part in the many forms of Daily Office available to the churches today.

The hymns are intended to be said to oneself as prayers, or sung quietly, either before or after the Office; or, if you want to include them in the Office itself, a suitable place would be before the psalms.

At the end of this book is a section of blank pages for your own personal material in the form of prayers, praises, or perhaps pictures.

MORNING CANTICLES

Venite (Psalm 95)

Come, let us sing to the Lord: let us shout for joy to the rock of our salvation.

Let us come before his presence with thanksgiving: and raise a loud shout to him with psalms.

For the Lord is a great God: and a great King above all gods.

In his hand are the depths of the earth: and the heights of the hills are his also.

The sea is his, for he made it: and his hands have molded the dry land.

Come, let us bow down and bend the knee: and kneel before the Lord our Maker.

For he is our God, and we are the people of his pasture, and the sheep of his hand: O that today you would hearken to his voice!

Harden not your hearts, as your forebears did in the wilderness: at Meribah and on that day at Massah, when they tempted me.

They put me to the test: though they had seen my works.

Forty years long I detested that generation and said: "This people are wayward in their hearts; they do not know my ways."

So I swore in my wrath: "They shall not enter my rest."

Jubilate (Psalm 100)

Be joyful in the Lord, all you lands: serve the Lord with gladness and come before his presence with a song.

Know this, the Lord himself is God: he himself has made us and we are his; we are his people and the sheep of his pasture.

Enter his gates with thanksgiving, go into his courts with praise: give thanks to him and call upon his name.

For the Lord is good, his mercy is everlasting: and his faithfulness endures from age to age.

Te Deum Laudamus

We praise you, O God: we acclaim you as the Lord;
All creation worships you: the Father everlasting.

To you all angels, all the powers of heaven: the cherubim and seraphim, sing in endless praise,

Holy, holy, holy Lord, God of power and might: heaven and earth are full of your glory,

The glorious company of apostles praise you: the noble fellowship of prophets praise you.

The white-robed army of martyrs praise you: throughout the world, the holy Church acclaims you.

Father, of majesty unbounded: your true and only Son, worthy of all praise; the Holy Spirit, advocate and guide.

You, Christ, are the King of glory: the eternal Son of the Father.

When you took our flesh to set us free: you humbly chose the virgin's womb.

You overcame the sting of death: and opened the kingdom of heaven to all believers.

You are seated at God's right hand in glory: we believe that you will come to be our judge.

Come then, Lord, and help your people, bought with the price of your own blood: and bring us with your saints to glory everlasting.

Benedicite Omnia Opera

Bless the Lord, all created things: who is worthy to be praised and exalted for ever.

Bless the Lord, you heavens: who is worthy to be praised and exalted for ever.

Bless the Lord, you angels of the Lord, bless the Lord, all you his hosts: bless the Lord, you waters above the heavens, who is worthy to be praised and exalted for ever.

Bless the Lord, sun and moon, bless the Lord, you stars of heaven: bless the Lord, all rain and dew, who is worthy to be praised and exalted for ever.

Bless the Lord, all winds that blow, bless the Lord, you fire and heat: bless the Lord, scorching wind and bitter cold, who is worthy to be praised and exalted for ever.

Bless the Lord, dews and falling snows, bless the Lord, you nights and days: bless the Lord, light and darkness, who is worthy to be praised and exalted for ever.

Bless the Lord, frost and cold, bless the Lord, you ice and snow: bless the Lord, lightning and clouds, who is worthy to be praised and exalted for ever.

O let the earth bless the Lord; bless the Lord, you mountains and hills: bless the Lord, all that grows in the ground, who is worthy to be praised and exalted for ever.

Bless the Lord, you springs, bless the Lord, you seas and rivers: bless the Lord, you whales and all that swim in the waters, who is worthy to be praised and exalted for ever.

Bless the Lord, all birds of the air, bless the Lord, you beasts and cattle: bless the Lord, all people of the earth, who is worthy to be praised and exalted for ever.

O people of God, bless the Lord; bless the Lord, you priests of the Lord: bless the Lord, you servants of the Lord, who is worthy to be praised and exalted for ever.

Bless the Lord, all you of upright spirit, bless the Lord, you that are holy and humble in heart: bless the Father, the Son and the Holy Spirit, who is worthy to be praised and exalted for ever.

Benedictus

Blessed be the Lord, the God of Israel: for he has come to his people and set them free.

He has raised up for us a mighty Savior: born of the house of his servant, David.

Through his holy prophets he promised of old: that he would save us from our enemies, from the hands of all that hate us.

He promised to show mercy to our forebears: and to remember his holy covenant.

This was the oath he swore to our father Abraham: to set us free from the hands of our enemies,

Free to worship him without fear: holy and righteous in his sight, all the days of our life.

You, my child, shall be called the prophet of the Most High: for you will go before the Lord to prepare his way,

To give his people knowledge of salvation: by the forgiveness of all their sins.

In the tender compassion of our God: the dawn from on high shall break upon us,

To shine on those who dwell in darkness and the shadow of death: and to guide our feet into the way of peace.

EVENING CANTICLES

Magnificat

My soul proclaims the greatness of the Lord: my spirit rejoices in God my Savior.

For he has looked with favor on his lowly servant: from this day all generations will call me blessed.

The Almighty has done great things for me: and holy is his name.

He has mercy on those who fear him: in every generation.

He has shown the strength of his arm: he has scattered the proud in their conceit.

He has cast down the mighty from their thrones: and has lifted up the lowly.

He has filled the hungry with good things: and the rich he has sent away empty.

He has come to the help of his servant, Israel: for he has remembered his promise of mercy.

The promise he made to our forebears: to Abraham and his children for ever.

Nunc Dimittis

Now, Lord, you let your servant go in peace: your word has been fulfilled.

My own eyes have seen the salvation: which you have prepared in the sight of every people;

A light to reveal you to the nations: and the glory of your people Israel.

EASTER ANTHEMS

Christ our Passover has been sacrificed for us:
so let us celebrate the feast,
　Not with the old leaven of corruption and
wickedness: but with the unleavened bread of
sincerity and truth.

　Christ once raised from the dead dies no more:
death has no more dominion over him.
　In dying he died to sin once for all: in living he
lives to God.
　See yourselves therefore as dead to sin: and alive
to God in Jesus Christ our Lord.

　Christ has been raised from the dead: the first-
fruits of those who sleep.
　For since by man came death: by man has come
also the resurrection of the dead.
　For as in Adam all die: even so in Christ shall all
be made alive.

FOR TIMES OF PRAISE

Gloria in Excelsis

Glory to God in the highest: and peace to his people on earth.

Lord God, heavenly King: almighty God and Father,

We worship you, we give you thanks: we praise you for your glory.

Lord Jesus Christ, only Son of the Father: Lord God, Lamb of God,

You take away the sin of the world: have mercy on us;

You are seated at the right hand of the Father: receive our prayer.

For you alone are the Holy One: you alone are the Lord,

You alone are the most high: Jesus Christ, with the Holy Spirit, in the glory of God the Father. Amen.

FOR TIMES OF REMEMBRANCE
OR BEREAVEMENT

Justorum Autem Animae

The souls of the righteous are in the hand of God: and no torment will ever touch them.

In the eyes of the foolish, they seem to have died: but they are at peace.

For though, in the sight of others, they were punished: their hope is of immortality.

Having been disciplined a little, they will receive great good: because God tested them and found them worthy.

Like gold in the furnace, God tried them: and, like a sacrificial burnt offering, accepted them.

In the time of their visitation they will shine forth: and will run like sparks through the stubble.

They will govern nations and rule over peoples: and God will reign over them for ever.

FOR TIMES OF PENITENCE

Salvator Mundi

Jesus, Savior of the world,
  come to us in your mercy:
we look to you to save and help us.

By your cross and your life laid down,
  you set your people free:
we look to you to save and help us.

When they were ready to perish
  you saved your disciples:
we look to you to come to our help.

In the greatness of your mercy,
  loose us from our chains:
forgive the sins of all your people.

Make yourself known
  as our savior and mighty deliverer:
save and help us that we may praise you.

Come now and dwell with us, Lord Christ Jesus:
hear our prayer and be with us always.

And when you come in your glory:
make us to be one with you
and to share the life of your kingdom.

FOR TIMES OF WONDER

Manifestum Est

Christ Jesus was revealed in the flesh: and
  vindicated in the Spirit.
He was seen by angels: and proclaimed among the
  nations.
Believed in throughout the world:
  he was taken up in glory.

PRAYERS AND MEDITATIONS

My hope is the Father, my refuge is the Son, my
protection is the Holy Spirit. Holy Trinity, glory to
thee. Amen.   *—Orthodox liturgy*

Glory

What shall I give you, Lord, in return for all this
  kindness?

Glory to you for your love.

Glory to you for your patience.

Glory to you for forgiving us all our sins.

Glory to you for coming to save our souls.

Glory to you for your incarnation in the virgin's
  womb.

Glory to you for your bonds.

Glory to you for receiving the cut of the lash.

Glory to you for accepting mockery.

Glory to you for your crucifixion.

Glory to you for your burial.

Glory to you for your resurrection.

Glory to you that were preached to men.

Glory to you in whom they believed.

Glory to you that were taken up into heaven.

                          —Ephrem the Syrian

The Divine Praises

Blessed be God.
Blessed be the holy and undivided Trinity.
Blessed be God the Father, maker of heaven and earth.
Blessed be Jesus Christ, truly divine and truly human.
Blessed be the holy Name of Jesus.
Blessed be Jesus Christ in his death and resurrection.
Blessed be Jesus Christ on his throne of glory.
Blessed be Jesus Christ in the sacrament of his
   body and blood.
Blessed be God the Holy Spirit, the giver and
   sustainer of life.
Blessed be God in the Virgin Mary, Mother of our
   Lord and God.
Blessed be God in the angels and saints.
Blessed be God.

The Cross

We glory in your cross, O Lord,
   and praise and glorify your holy resurrection:
for by virtue of the cross,
   joy has come to the whole world.

* * *

In times of pain and grief he shows us the joy with which he embraced his own cross and passion, at the same time helping us to bear our troubles by his blessed strength. And in times of sin his compassion and pity are there to cheer us, powerfully protecting us against all enemies. These two are the everyday comforts he shows us in this life.

–Julian of Norwich

* * *

The cross is the way of the lost.
The cross is the staff of the lame.
The cross is the guide of the blind.
The cross is the strength of the weak.
The cross is the hope of the hopeless.
The cross is the freedom of slaves.
The cross is the water of the seeds.
The cross is the consolation of the bonded laborers.
The cross is the source of those who seek water.
The cross is the cloth of the naked.

–Tenth-century African hymn

Celtic Journey Blessing

Bless to me, O God,   The earth beneath my foot,
Bless to me, O God,   The path whereon I go;
Bless to me, O God,   The thing of my desire;

Thou Evermore of evermore,
Bless Thou to me my rest.

Bless to me the thing   Whereon is set my mind,
Bless to me the thing   Whereon is set my love;
Bless to me the thing   Whereon is set my hope;

O Thou King of kings,
Bless Thou to me mine eye!

Celtic Prayer for Protection

O holy God of truth,   O loving God of mercy
Sign me from the spells, Sign me from the charms.

Compassionate God of life, Forgiveness to me give
In my wanton talk,
In my lying oath,
In my foolish deed,
In my empty speech.

Collect for Purity

Almighty God, to whom all hearts are open, all desires known, and from whom no secrets are hidden: cleanse the thoughts of our hearts by the inspiration of your Holy Spirit, that we may perfectly love you, and worthily magnify your holy name; through Christ our Lord.

The Yoke of Obedience

I am no longer my own, but yours. Put me to what you will, rank me with whom you will; put me to doing, put me to suffering; let me be employed for you or laid aside for you, exalted for you or brought low for you; let me be full, let me be empty; let me have all things, let me have nothing; I freely and wholeheartedly yield all things to your pleasure and disposal. And now, glorious and blessed God, Father, Son, and Holy Spirit, you are mine and I am yours. So be it. And the Covenant now made on earth, let it be ratified in heaven.

–*The Covenant Service of the Methodist Church*

Anima Christi

Soul of Christ, sanctify me,
Body of Christ, save me,
Blood of Christ, flood me,

Water from the side of Christ, wash me.
O good Jesu, hear me,
Within thy wounds hide me,
Suffer me not to be separated from thee,
From the malicious enemy defend me,
In the hour of my death call me,
And bid me come to thee,
That with thy saints I may praise thee,
forever and ever.

The Rosary

The Rosary, the Angelus, and the brief Prayer to Our Lady can be used by all Christians who see in Mary a model of what it is to bear God's Word. They encompass the mystery of the incarnation, cross, and resurrection and point to the completion of God's purpose in our lives.

The Joyful Mysteries

The Annunciation, The Visitation, The Nativity, The Presentation in the Temple, The Finding of the Child Jesus.

The Sorrowful Mysteries

The Agony in the Garden, The Scourging at the Pillar, The Crowning with Thorns, The Carrying of the Cross, The Crucifixion.

The Glorious Mysteries

The Resurrection, The Ascension, The Descent of the Holy Spirit, The Assumption of Mary, The Coronation of Mary.

The Angelus

The angel of the Lord brought tidings to Mary:
And she conceived by the Holy Ghost.

Hail, Mary, fall of grace, the Lord is with thee:
Blessed art thou among women, and blessed is the
  fruit of thy womb, Jesus.
Behold the handmaid of the Lord:
Be it unto me according to your word.

Hail, Mary . . .

And the Word was made flesh:
And dwelt among us.

Hail, Mary . . .

Pray for us, O holy Mother of God:
That we may be made worthy of the promises of
  Christ.

We beseech thee, O Lord, to pour thy grace into our hearts, that as we have known the incarnation of thy Son Jesus Christ by the message of an angel, so by his cross and passion we may be brought to the glory of his resurrection, through the same Christ our Lord.

Prayer to Our Lady

Our Lady, our Queen and our Mother, in the name of Jesus and for the love of Jesus, we implore thee to take our cause in hand and to grant us good success.

Prayer to St. Michael

Holy Michael, Archangel, defend us in the day of battle; be our safeguard against the wickedness and snares of the devil. May God rebuke him, we humbly pray: and do thou, prince of the heavenly host, by the power of God thrust down to hell Satan, and all other wicked spirits who wander through the world for the ruin of souls.

The Morning Star

Christ is the morning star who, when the night of this world is past, brings to his saints the promise of the light of life and opens everlasting day.

—Venerable Bede

ADDITIONAL PSALMS

Additional psalms may be said after the main psalms.

Psalm 4

Answer me when I call, O God, defender of my cause: you set me free when I am hard-pressed; have mercy upon me and hear my prayer.

"You mortals, how long will you dishonor my glory: how long will you worship dumb idols, and run after false gods?"

Know that the Lord does wonders for the faithful: when I call upon the Lord, he will hear me.

Tremble, then, and do not sin: speak to your heart in silence upon your bed.

Offer the appointed sacrifices: and put your trust in the Lord.

Many are saying, "O that we might see better times": Lift up the light of your countenance upon us, O Lord.

You have put gladness in my heart: more than when grain and wine and oil increase.

I lie down in peace; at once I fall asleep: for only you, Lord, make me dwell in safety.

Psalm 8

O Lord, our governor: how exalted is your name in all the world!

Out of the mouths of infants and children: your majesty is praised above the heavens.

You have set up a stronghold against your adversaries: to quell the enemy and the avenger.

When I consider your heavens, the work of your fingers: the moon and the stars you have set in their courses,

What are mortals, that you should be mindful of them: mere human beings, that you should seek them out?

You have made them little lower than the angels: you adorn them with glory and honor.

You give them mastery over the works of your hands: and put all things under their feet,

All sheep and oxen: even the wild beasts of the field,

The birds of the air, the fish of the sea: and whatsoever walks in the paths of the sea.

O Lord, our governor: how exalted is your name in all the world!

Psalm 11

In the Lord have I taken refuge: how then can you say to me, "Fly away like a bird to the hilltop;

"For see how the wicked bend the bow, and fit their arrows to the string: to shoot from ambush at the true of heart.

"When the foundations are being destroyed: what can the righteous do?"

The Lord is in his holy temple: the Lord's throne is in heaven.

His eyes behold the inhabited world: his piercing eye weighs our worth.

The Lord weighs the righteous as well as the wicked: but those who delight in violence he abhors.

Upon the wicked he shall rain coals of fire and burning sulphur: a scorching wind shall be their lot.

For the Lord is righteous; he delights in righteous deeds: and the just shall see his face.

Psalm 16

Protect me, O God, for I take refuge in you: I have said to the Lord, "You are my Lord, my good above all other."

All my delight is upon the godly that are in the land: upon those who are noble among the people.

But those who run after other gods: shall have their troubles multiplied.

Their libations of blood I will not offer: nor take the names of their gods upon my lips.

O Lord, you are my portion and my cup: it is you who uphold my lot.

My boundaries enclose a pleasant land: indeed, I have a goodly heritage.

I will bless the Lord who gives me counsel: my heart teaches me, night after night.

I have set the Lord always before me: because he is at my right hand I shall not fall.

My heart, therefore, is glad, and my spirit rejoices: my body also shall rest in hope.

For you will not abandon me to the grave: nor let your holy one see the Pit.

You will show me the path of life: in your presence there is fullness of joy, and in your right hand are pleasures for evermore.

Psalm 19

The heavens declare the glory of God: and the firmament shows his handiwork.

One day tells its tale to another: and one night imparts knowledge to another.

Although they have no words or language: and their voices are not heard,

Their sound has gone out into all lands: and their message to the ends of the world.

In the deep he has set a pavilion for the sun: it

comes out like a bridegroom out of his chamber; it rejoices like a champion to run its course.

It goes forth from the uttermost edge of the heavens, and runs about to the end of it again: nothing is hidden from its burning heat.

The law of the Lord is perfect and revives the soul: the testimony of the Lord is sure and gives wisdom to the innocent.

The statutes of the Lord are just and rejoice the heart: the commandment of the Lord is clear and gives light to the eyes.

The fear of the Lord is clean and endures for ever: the judgments of the Lord are true and righteous altogether.

More to be desired are they than gold, more than much fine gold: sweeter far than honey, than honey in the comb.

By them also is your servant enlightened: and in keeping of them there is great reward.

Who can tell how often he offends: cleanse me from my secret faults.

Above all, keep your servant from presumptuous sins; let them not get dominion over me: then shall I be whole and sound, and innocent of a great offense.

Let the words of my mouth and the meditation of my heart be acceptable in your sight: O Lord, my strength and my redeemer.

Psalm 22

My God, my God, why have you forsaken me: and are so far from my cry and from the words of my distress?

O my God, I cry in the daytime, but you do not answer: by night as well, but I find no rest.

Yet you are the holy one: enthroned upon the praises of Israel.

Our forebears put their trust in you: they trusted and you delivered them.

They cried out to you and were delivered: they trusted in you and were not put to shame.

But as for me, I am a worm and no man: scorned by all and despised by the people.

All who see me laugh me to scorn: they curl their lips and wag their heads, saying,

"He trusted in the Lord; let him deliver him: let him rescue him, if he delights in him."

Yet you are he who took me out of the womb: and kept me safe upon my mother's breast.

I have been entrusted to you ever since I was born: you were my God when I was still in my mother's womb.

Be not far from me, for trouble is near: and there is none to help.

Many young bulls encircle me: strong bulls of Bashan surround me.

They open wide their jaws at me: like a ravening and roaring lion.

I am poured out like water, all my bones are out of joint: my heart within my breast is melting wax.

My mouth is dried up like a potsherd; my tongue sticks to the roof of my mouth: and you have laid me in the dust of the grave.

Packs of dogs close me in, and gangs of evildoers circle around me: they pierce my hands and feet; I can count all my bones.

They stare and gloat over me: they divide my garments among them; they cast lots for my clothing.

Be not far from me, O Lord: you are my strength; hasten to help me.

Save me from the sword: my life from the power of the dog!

Save me from the lion's mouth: my wretched body from the horns of wild bulls.

I will declare your name to my people: in the midst of the congregation I will praise you.

Praise the Lord, you that fear him: stand in awe of him, O offspring of Israel; all you of Jacob's line, give him glory.

For he does not despise or abhor the poor in their poverty; neither does he hide his face from them: but when they cry to him he hears them.

My praise is of him in the great assembly: I will perform my vows in the presence of those who worship him.

The poor shall eat and be satisfied; those who seek the Lord shall praise him: "May your heart live for ever!"

All the ends of the earth shall remember and turn to the Lord: and all the families of the nations shall bow before him.

For kingship belongs to the Lord: he rules over the nations.

To him alone all who sleep in the earth bow down in worship: all who go down to the dust fall before him.

My soul shall live for him; my descendants shall serve him: they shall be known as the Lord's for ever.

They shall come and make known to a people yet unborn: the saving deeds that he has done.

Psalm 23

The Lord is my shepherd: I shall not be in want.

He makes me lie down in green pastures: and leads me beside still waters.

He revives my soul: and guides me along right pathways for his name's sake.

Though I walk through the valley of the shadow of death, I shall fear no evil: for you are with me; your rod and your staff, they comfort me.

You spread a table before me in the presence of those who trouble me: you have anointed my head with oil, and my cup is running over.

Surely your goodness and mercy shall follow me all the days of my life: and I will dwell in the house of the Lord for ever.

Psalm 23 (Prayer Book Version)

The Lord is my shepherd: therefore can I lack nothing.

He shall feed me in a green pasture: and lead me forth beside the waters of comfort.

He shall convert my soul: and bring me forth in the paths of righteousness, for his name's sake.

Yea, though I walk through the valley of the shadow of death, I will fear no evil: for thou art with me; thy rod and thy staff comfort me.

Thou shalt prepare a table before me against them that trouble me: thou hast anointed my head with oil, and my cup shall be full.

But thy loving-kindness and mercy shall follow me all the days of my life: and I will dwell in the house of the Lord for ever.

Psalm 24

The earth is the Lord's and all that is in it: the world and all who dwell therein,

For it is he who founded it upon the seas: and made it firm upon the rivers of the deep.

"Who can ascend the hill of the Lord: and who can stand in his holy place?"

"Those who have clean hands and a pure heart: who have not pledged themselves to falsehood, nor sworn by what is a fraud.

"They shall receive a blessing from the Lord: and a just reward from the God of their salvation."

Such is the generation of those who seek him: of those who seek your face, O God of Jacob.

Lift up your heads, O gates; lift them high, O everlasting doors: and the King of glory shall come in.

"Who is this King of glory?": "The Lord, strong and mighty, the Lord, mighty in battle."

Lift up your heads, O gates; lift them high, O everlasting doors: and the King of glory shall come in.

"Who is he, this King of glory?": "The Lord of hosts, he is the King of glory."

Psalm 27

The Lord is my light and my salvation; whom then shall I fear: the Lord is the strength of my life; of whom then shall I be afraid?

When evildoers came upon me to eat up my flesh: it was they, my foes and my adversaries, who stumbled and fell.

Though an army should encamp against me: yet my heart shall not be afraid;

And though war should rise up against me: yet will I put my trust in him.

One thing have I asked of the Lord, one thing I seek: that I may dwell in the house of the Lord all the days of my life;

To behold the fair beauty of the Lord: and to seek him in his temple.

For in the day of trouble he shall keep me safe in his shelter: he shall hide me in the secrecy of his dwelling and set me high upon a rock.

Even now he lifts up my head: above my enemies round about me;

Therefore I will offer in his dwelling an oblation with sounds of great gladness: I will sing and make music to the Lord.

Hearken to my voice, O Lord, when I call: have mercy on me and answer me.

You speak in my heart and say, "Seek my face": your face, Lord, will I seek.

Hide not your face from me: nor turn away your servant in displeasure.

You have been my helper; cast me not away: do not forsake me, O God of my salvation.

Though my father and my mother forsake me: the Lord will sustain me.

Show me your way, O Lord: lead me on a level path, because of my enemies.

Deliver me not into the hand of my adversaries: for false witnesses have risen up against me, and also those who speak malice.

What if I had not believed that I should see the goodness of the Lord: in the land of the living!

O tarry and await the Lord's pleasure; be strong and he shall comfort your heart: wait patiently for the Lord.

Psalm 39

I said, "I will keep watch upon my ways: so that I do not offend with my tongue.

"I will put a muzzle on my mouth: while the wicked are in my presence."

So I held my tongue and said nothing: I refrained from rash words; but my pain became unbearable.

My heart was hot within me; while I pondered the fire burst into flame: I spoke Out with my tongue: —

Lord, let me know my end and the number of my days: so that I may know how short my life is.

You have given me a mere handful of days, and my lifetime is as nothing in your sight: truly even those who stand erect are but a puff of wind.

We walk about like a shadow and in vain are we in turmoil: we heap up riches and cannot tell who will gather them.

And now, what is my hope?: O Lord, my hope is in you.

Deliver me from all my transgressions: and do not make me the taunt of the fool.

I fell silent and did not open my mouth: for surely it was you that did it.

Take your affliction from me: I am worn down by the blows of your hand.

With rebukes for sin you punish us; like a moth you eat away all that is dear to us: truly everyone is but a puff of wind.

Hear my prayer, O Lord, and give ear to my cry: hold not your peace at my tears.

For I am but a sojourner with you: a wayfarer, as all my forebears were.

Turn your gaze from me, that I may be glad again: before I go my way and am no more.

Psalm 42

As the deer longs for the water-brooks: so longs my soul for you, O God.

My soul is athirst for God, athirst for the living God: when shall I come to appear before the presence of God?

My tears have been my food day and night: while all day long they say to me, "Where is now your God?"

I pour out my soul while I think on these things: how I went with the multitude and led them to the house of God,

With the voice of praise and thanksgiving: among those who keep holy-day.

Why are you so full of heaviness, O my soul: and why are you so disquieted within me?

Put your trust in God: for I will yet give thanks to him, who is the help of my countenance and my God.

My soul is heavy within me: therefore I will remember you from the land of Jordan, and from the peak of Mizar among the heights of Hermon.

One deep calls to another in the noise of your cataracts: all your rapids and floods have gone over me.

The Lord grants his loving-kindness in the day-time: in the night season his song is with me, a prayer to the God of my life.

I will say to the God of my strength, "Why have you forgotten me: and why do I go so heavily while the enemy oppresses me?"

While my bones are being broken: my enemies mock me to my face;

All day long they mock me: say to me, "Where is now your God?"

Why are you so full of heaviness, O my soul: and why are you so disquieted within me?

Put your trust in God: for I will yet give thanks to him, who is the help of my countenance and my God.

Psalm 46

God is our refuge and strength: a very present help in trouble;

Therefore we will not fear, though the earth be moved: and though the mountains be toppled into the depths of the sea;

Though its waters rage and foam: and though the mountains tremble at its tumult.

The Lord of hosts is with us: the God of Jacob is our stronghold.

There is a river whose streams make glad the city of God: the holy habitation of the Most High.

God is in the midst of her; she shall not be overthrown: God shall help her at the break of day.

The nations make much ado and the kingdoms are shaken: God has spoken and the earth shall melt away.

The Lord of hosts is with us: the God of Jacob is our stronghold.

Come now and look upon the works of the Lord: what awesome things he has done on earth.

It is he who makes war to cease in all the world: he breaks the bow and shatters the spear, and burns the shields with fire.

"Be still, then, and know that I am God: I will be exalted among the nations; I will be exalted in the earth."

The Lord of hosts is with us: the God of Jacob is our stronghold.

Psalm 63

O God, you are my God; eagerly I seek you: my soul thirsts for you, my flesh faints for you, as in a barren and dry land where there is no water;

Therefore I have gazed upon you in your holy place: that I might behold your power and your glory.

For your loving-kindness is better than life itself: my lips shall give you praise.

So I will bless you as long as I live: and lift up my hands in your name.

My soul is content, as with marrow and fatness: and my mouth praises you with joyful lips,

When I remember you upon my bed: and meditate upon you in the night watches.

For you have been my helper: and under the shadow of your wings I will rejoice.

My soul clings to you: your right hand holds me fast.

May those who seek my life to destroy it: go down into the depths of the earth;

Let them fall upon the edge of the sword: and let them be food for jackals.

But the king will rejoice in God; all those who swear by him will be glad: for the mouth of those who speak lies shall be stopped.

Psalm 67

May God be merciful to us and bless us: show us the light of his countenance and come to us.

Let your ways be known upon earth: your saving health among all nations.

Let the peoples praise you, O God: let all the peoples praise you.

Let the nations be glad and sing for joy: for you judge the peoples with equity and guide all the nations upon earth.

Let the peoples praise you, O God: let all the peoples praise you.

The earth has brought forth her increase: may God, our own God, give us his blessing.

May God give us his blessing: and may all the ends of the earth stand in awe of him.

Psalm 84

How dear to me is your dwelling, O Lord of hosts!: my soul has a desire and longing for the courts of the Lord; my heart and my flesh rejoice in the living God.

The sparrow has found her a house and the swallow a nest where she may lay her young: by the side of your altars, O Lord of hosts, my king and my God.

Happy are they who dwell in your house: they will always be praising you.

Happy are the people whose strength is in you: whose hearts are set on the pilgrims' way.

Those who go through the desolate valley will find it a place of springs: for the early rains have covered it with pools of water.

They will climb from height to height: and the God of gods will reveal himself in Zion.

Lord God of hosts, hear my prayer: hearken, O God of Jacob.

Behold our defender, O God: and look upon the face of your anointed,

For one day in your courts is better than a thousand in my own room: and to stand at the threshold of the house of my God is better than to dwell in the tents of the wicked,

For the Lord God is both a sun and a shield: he will give grace and glory;

No good thing will the Lord withhold: from those who walk with integrity.

O Lord of hosts: happy are they who put their trust in you!

Psalm 88

O Lord, my God, my Savior: by day and night I cry to you.

Let my prayer enter into your presence: incline your ear to my lamentation.

For I am full of trouble: my life is at the brink of the grave.

I am counted among those who go down to the Pit: I have become like one who has no strength;

Lost among the dead: like the slain who lie in the grave,

Whom you remember no more: for they are cut off from your hand.

You have laid me in the depths of the Pit: in dark places and in the abyss.

Your anger weighs upon me heavily: and all your great waves overwhelm me.

You have put my friends far from me; you have made me to be abhorred by them: I am in prison and cannot get free.

My sight has failed me because of trouble: Lord, I have called upon you daily; I have stretched out my hands to you.

Do you work wonders for the dead: will those who have died stand up to give you thanks?

Will your loving-kindness be declared in the grave: your faithfulness in the land of destruction?

Will your wonders be known in the dark: or your righteousness in the country where all is forgotten?

But as for me, O Lord, I cry to you for help: in the morning my prayer comes before you.

Lord, why have you rejected me: and why have you hidden your face from me?

Ever since my youth, I have been wretched and at the point of death: I have borne your terrors with a troubled mind.

Your blazing anger has swept over me: your terrors have destroyed me;

They surround me all day long like a flood: they encompass me on every side.

My friend and neighbor you have put away from me: and darkness is my only companion.

Psalm 90

Lord, you have been our refuge: from one generation to another.

Before the mountains were brought forth, or the land and the earth were born: from age to age you are God.

You turn us back to the dust and say: "Go back, O child of earth."

For a thousand years in your sight are like yesterday when it is past: and like a watch in the night.

You sweep us away like a dream: we fade away suddenly like the grass.

In the morning it is green and flourishes: in the evening it is dried up and withered.

For we are consumed by your displeasure: we are afraid because of your wrathful indignation.

Our iniquities you have set before you: and our secret sins in the light of your countenance.

When you are angry, all our days are gone: we bring our years to an end with a sigh.

The span of our life is seventy years, perhaps in strength even eighty: yet the sum of them is but labor and sorrow, for they pass away quickly and we are gone.

Who regards the power of your wrath: who rightly fears your indignation?

So teach us to number our days: so that we apply our hearts to wisdom.

Return, O Lord; how long will you tarry?: be gracious to your servants.

Satisfy us by your loving-kindness in the morning: so shall we rejoice and be glad all the days of our life.

Make us glad by the measure of the days that you afflicted us: and the years in which we suffered adversity.

Show your servants your works: and your splendor to your children.

May the graciousness of the Lord our God be upon us: prosper the work of our hands; prosper our handiwork.

Psalm 91

He who dwells in the shelter of the Most High: abides under the shadow of the Almighty.

He shall say to the Lord, "You are my refuge and my stronghold: my God in whom I put my trust."

He shall deliver you from the snare of the hunter: and from the deadly pestilence.

He shall cover you with his pinions, and you shall find refuge under his wings: his faithfulness shall be a shield and buckler.

You shall not be afraid of any terror by night: nor of the arrow that flies by day;

Of the plague that stalks in the darkness: nor of the sickness that lays waste at mid-day.

A thousand shall fall at your side and ten thousand at your right hand: but it shall not come near you.

Your eyes have only to behold: to see the reward of the wicked,

Because you have made the Lord your refuge: and the Most High your habitation,

There shall no evil happen to you: neither shall any plague come near your dwelling,

For he shall give his angels charge over you: to keep you in all your ways.

They shall bear you in their hands: lest you dash your foot against a stone.

You shall tread upon the lion and adder: you shall trample the young lion and the serpent under your feet.

Because he is bound to me in love, therefore will I deliver him: I will protect him, because he knows my name.

He shall call upon me and I will answer him: I am with him in trouble, I will rescue him and bring him to honor.

With long life will I satisfy him: and show him my salvation.

Psalm 103

Bless the Lord, O my soul: and all that is within me, bless his holy name.

Bless the Lord, O my soul: and forget not all his benefits.

He forgives all your sins: and heals all your infirmities;

He redeems your life from the grave: and crowns you with mercy and loving-kindness;

He satisfies you with good things: and your youth is renewed like an eagle's.

The Lord executes righteousness: and judgment for all who are oppressed.

He made his ways known to Moses: and his works to the children of Israel.

The Lord is full of compassion and mercy: slow to anger and of great kindness.

He will not always accuse us: nor will he keep his anger for ever.

He has not dealt with us according to our sins: nor rewarded us according to our wickedness.

For as the heavens are high above the earth: so is his mercy great upon those who fear him.

As far as the east is from the west: so far has he removed our sins from us.

As a father cares for his children: so does the Lord care for those who fear him.

For he himself knows whereof we are made: he remembers that we are but dust.

Our days are like the grass: we flourish like a flower of the field;

When the wind goes over it, it is gone: and its place shall know it no more.

But the merciful goodness of the Lord endures for ever on those who fear him: and his righteousness on children's children;

On those who keep his covenant: and remember his commandments and do them.

The Lord has set his throne in heaven: and his kingship has dominion over all.

Bless the Lord, you angels of his, you mighty

ones who do his bidding: and hearken to the voice of his word.

Bless the Lord, all you his hosts: you ministers of his who do his will.

Bless the Lord, all you works of his, in all places of his dominion: bless the Lord, O my soul.

Psalm 114

When Israel came out of Egypt: the house of Jacob from a people of strange speech,

Judah became God's sanctuary: and Israel his dominion.

The sea beheld it and fled: Jordan turned and went back.

The mountains skipped like rams: and the little hills like young sheep.

What ailed you, O sea, that you fled: O Jordan, that you turned back?

You mountains, that you skipped like rams: you little hills like young sheep?

Tremble, O earth, at the presence of the Lord: at the presence of the God of Jacob.

Who turned the hard rock into a pool of water: and flint-stone into a flowing spring.

Psalm 130

Out of the depths have I called to you, O Lord;
Lord, hear my voice: O let your ears consider well
the voice of my supplication.

If you, Lord, were to note what is done amiss: O
Lord, who could stand?

For there is forgiveness with you: therefore you
shall be feared.

I wait for the Lord, my soul waits for him: in his
word is my hope.

My soul waits for the Lord: more than the night-
watch for the morning, more than the night-watch
for the morning.

O Israel, wait for the Lord: for with the Lord
there is mercy,

With him is plenteous redemption: and he shall
redeem Israel from all their sins.

Psalm 134

Behold now bless the Lord, all you servants of the
Lord: you that stand by night in the house of the
Lord.

Lift up your hands in the holy place and bless the
Lord: the Lord who made heaven and earth bless
you out of Zion.

Psalm 139

Lord, you have searched me out and known me:
you know my sitting down and my rising up; you
discern my thoughts from afar.

You trace my journeys and my resting places:
and are acquainted with all my ways.

Indeed there is not a word on my lips: but you,
O Lord, know it altogether.

You press upon me behind and before: and lay
your hand upon me.

Such knowledge is too wonderful for me: it is so
high that I cannot attain to it.

Where can I go then from your Spirit: where can
I flee from your presence?

If I climb up to heaven, you are there: if I make
the grave my bed, you are there also.

If I take the wings of the morning: and dwell in
the uttermost parts of the sea,

Even there your hand will lead me: and your
right hand hold me fast.

If I say, "Surely the darkness will cover me: and
the light around me turn to night,"

Darkness is not dark to you; the night is as bright
as the day: darkness and light to you are both alike.

For you yourself created my inmost parts: you
knit me together in my mother's womb.

I will thank you because I am marvelously made:
your works are wonderful and I know it well.

My body was not hidden from you: while I was being made in secret, and woven in the depths of the earth.

Your eyes beheld my limbs, yet unfinished in the womb; all of them were written in your book: they were fashioned day by day, when as yet there was none of them.

How deep I find your thoughts, O God: how great is the sum of them!

If I were to count them, they would be more in number than the sand: to count them all, my life span would need to be like yours.

O that you would slay the wicked, O God: you that thirst for blood, depart from me.

They speak despitefully against you: your enemies take your name in vain.

Do I not hate those, O Lord, who hate you: and do I not loathe those who rise up against you?

I hate them with perfect hatred: they have become my own enemies.

Search me out, O God, and know my heart: try me and know my restless thoughts.

Look well whether there be any wickedness in me: and lead me in the way that is everlasting.

Psalm 148

Alleluia! Praise the Lord from the heavens: praise him in the heights.

Praise him, all you angels of his: praise him, all his host.

Praise him, sun and moon: praise him, all you shining stars.

Praise him, heaven of heavens: and you waters above the heavens.

Let them praise the name of the Lord: for he commanded and they were created.

He made them stand fast for ever and ever: he gave them a law which shall not pass away.

Praise the Lord from the earth: you sea monsters and all deeps;

Fire and hail, snow and fog: tempestuous wind, doing his will;

Mountains and all hills: fruit trees and all cedars;

Wild beasts and all cattle: creeping things and winged birds;

Kings of the earth and all peoples: princes and all rulers of the world;

Young men and maidens: old and young together.

Let them praise the name of the Lord: for his name only is exalted, his splendor is over earth and heaven.

He has raised up strength for his people and praise for all his loyal servants: the children of Israel, a people who are near him. Alleluia!

HYMNS TO BE USED AS PRAYERS

Nocte Surgentes

Father, we praise thee, now the night is over,
Active and watchful, stand we all before thee;
Singing we offer prayer and meditation:
Thus we adore thee.

Monarch of all things, fit us for thy mansions:
Banish our weakness, health and wholeness sending;
Bring us to heaven, where thy saints united
Joy without ending.

All-holy Father, Son and equal Spirit,
Trinity blessed, send us thy salvation;
Thine is the glory, gleaming and resounding
Through all creation.

Christ, Whose Glory Fills the Skies

Christ, whose glory fills the skies,
Christ the true, the only light,
Sun of righteousness, arise,
Triumph o'er the shades of night;
Dayspring from on high, be near;
Daystar, in my heart appear.

Dark and cheerless is the morn
Unaccompanied by thee;
Joyless is the day's return,
Till thy mercy's beams I see,
Till they inward light impart,
Glad my eyes, and warm my heart.

Visit then this soul of mine,
Pierce the gloom of sin and grief
Fill me, radiancy divine,
Scatter all my unbelief
More and more thyself display,
Shining to the perfect day.

St. Patrick's Breastplate

I bind unto myself today
The strong name of the Trinity,
By invocation of the same,
The Three in One and One in Three.

I bind this day to me for ever,
By power of faith, Christ's incarnation;
His baptism in the Jordan river;
His death on the cross for my salvation;
His bursting from the spiced tomb;
His riding up the heavenly way;
His coming at the day of doom;
I bind unto myself today.

I bind unto myself today
The virtues of the star-lit heaven,
The glorious sun's life-giving ray,
The whiteness of the moon at even,
The flashing of the lightning free,
The whirling wind's tempestuous shocks,
The stable earth, the deep salt sea,
Around the old eternal rocks.

I bind unto myself today
The power of God to hold and lead,
His eye to watch, his might to stay,
His ear to hearken to my need.
The wisdom of my God to teach,
His hand to guide, his shield to ward;
The Word of God to give me speech,
His heavenly host to be my guard.

Christ be with me, Christ within me,
Christ behind me, Christ before me,
Christ beside me, Christ to win me,
Christ to comfort and restore me,
Christ beneath me, Christ above me,
Christ in quiet, Christ in danger,
Christ in hearts of all that love me,
Christ in mouth of friend and stranger.

I bind unto myself the name,
The strong name of the Trinity,

By invocation of the same,
The Three in One and One in Three.
Of whom all nature hath creation,
Eternal Father, Spirit, Word;
Praise to the Lord of my salvation,
Salvation is of Christ the Lord.

Veni Sancte Spiritus

Come, thou holy Paraclete,
And from thy celestial seat
Send thy light and brilliancy:
Father of the poor, draw near;
Giver of all gifts, be here;
Come, the soul's true radiancy.

Come, of comforters the best,
Of the soul the sweetest guest,
Come in toil refreshingly;
Thou in labor rest most sweet,
Thou art shadow from the heat,
Comfort in adversity.

O thou light, most pure and blest,
Shine within the inmost breast
Of thy faithful company.
Where thou art not, man hath nought;
Every holy deed and thought
Comes from thy Divinity.

What is soiled make thou pure;
What is wounded work its cure;
What is parched fructify;
What is rigid gently bend;
What is frozen warmly tend;
Straighten what goes erringly.

Fill thy faithful, who confide
In thy power to guard and guide,
With thy sevenfold mystery.
Here thy grace and virtue send;
Grant salvation in the end,
And in heaven felicity.

Veni Creator Spiritus

Come, Holy Ghost, our souls inspire,
And lighten with celestial fire;
Thou the anointing Spirit art,
Who dost thy sevenfold gifts impart.

Thy blessed unction from above
Is comfort, life and fire of love.
Enable with perpetual light
The dullness of our blinded sight.

Anoint and cheer our soiled face
With the abundance of thy grace;

Keep far our foes, give peace at home;
Where thou art guide, no ill may come.

Teach us to know the Father, Son,
And thee, of both, to be but One,
That through the ages all along,
This may be our endless song:

Praise to thine eternal merit,
Father, Son and Holy Spirit.

O King, Enthroned on High
An Eastern hymn to the Holy Spirit

O King, enthroned on high,
Thou Comforter divine,
Blessed Spirit of all truth, be nigh
And make us thine.

Thou art the Source of life,
Thou art our treasure-store;
Give us thy peace, and end our strife
For evermore.

Descend, O heavenly Dove,
Abide with us alway;
And in the fullness of thy love
Cleanse us, we pray.

Phos Hilaron

two versions

Hail, gladdening Light, of his pure glory poured
Who is the immortal Father, heavenly, blest,
Holiest of holies, Jesus Christ the Lord!

Now we are come to the sun's hour of rest,
The lights of evening round us shine,
We hymn the Father, Son and Holy Spirit divine.

Worthiest art thou at all times to be sung
With undefiled tongue,
Son of our God, giver of life alone:
Therefore in all the world thy glories, Lord, they own.

* * *

Light of the world in grace and beauty,
Mirror of God's eternal face,
Transparent flame of love's free duty,
You bring salvation to our race.
Now as we see the lights of evening,
We raise our voice in hymns of praise;
Worthy are you of endless blessing,
Sun of our night, lamp of our days.

Evening Hymn

We praise you, Father, for your gift
Of dusk and nightfall over earth,
Foreshadowing the mystery
Of death that leads to endless day.

Within your hands we rest secure,
In quiet sleep our strength renew;
Yet give your people hearts that wake
In love to you, unsleeping Lord.

Your glory may we ever seek,
In rest as in activity,
Until its fullness is revealed,
O source of life, O Trinity.

PERSONAL MATERIAL

SOURCES

1 Scripture quotations from the *Revised Standard Version* of the Bible, copyright 1946, 1952, and 1971 by the Division of Christian Education of the National Council of the Churches of Christ in the USA. Used by permission.

2 Scripture quotations from the *New Revised Standard Version* of the Bible, copyright 1989 by the Division of Christian Education of the National Council of the Churches of Christ in the USA. All rights reserved. Used by permission.

3 Prayers from *Prayers for Use at the Alternative Services* compiled by David Silk (1980, revised 1986), © Cassell PLC, are reproduced by permission of the publisher (Mowbray, an imprint of Cassell PLC).

4 The collects for Epiphany 4, Pentecost 13, 14, 18, and Morning Prayer, the Collect for Purity, the Easter Anthems, and Savior of the World from *The Alternative Service Book 1980* are copyright © The Central Board of Finance of the Church of England. The text of the *Gloria in Excelsis* as it appears in the Order for Holy Communion Rite A is copyright © 1970, 1971, 1975 International Consultation on English Texts (ICET). The Lord's Prayer is in the modified traditional (Rite B) version. Reproduced by permission.

5 Material from *Celebrating Common Prayer* (Mowbray), © The Society of St. Francis 1992, is used with permission.

6 The English translations of the *Te Deum*, *Benedictus*, *Magnificat*, and *Nunc Dimittis* prepared by the English Language Liturgical Consultation (ELLC).

ACKNOWLEDGMENTS

The figures 1, 2, 3 etc. refer to the Sources listed above.

"The moon in Lleyn" from R. S. Thomas, *Collected Poems 1945–1990* (J. M. Dent). Used with permission.

"Look, Father, look . . ." from the hymn "And now, O Father, mindful of the love" by W. Bright.

Wisdom of Solomon 7:25–27 (RSV). *1*

Refrains on Psalms Pss. 31:15; 139:18; 36:9; 45:1; 23:1; 34:7; 27:1; 27:8.

Psalms 121 and *124* Text: *Book of Common Prayer of the Episcopal Church in the USA* (ECUSA), also used in *Celebrating Common Prayer* (CCP). The US Book of Common Prayer is not subject to copyright.

Psalm 126 Text is an adaptation of existing versions.

The Song of the Servant Text RSV. *1*

Canticle Refrains Habakkuk 3:2; Zechariah 4:6; 1 Corinthians 15:42; Matthew 7:7; Malachi 4:2; John 20:29; Colossians 1:27.

Canticle of Christ's Glory Philippians 2:5–11, version by the author.

The Wisdom of Jesus Text NRSV. 2

Collects Monday: Prayer of St Gregory Nazianzen. 3 Tuesday to Saturday: Collects for Pentecost 18, Morning Prayer, Epiphany 4, Pentecost 13, Pentecost 14 (ASB). 4 Sunday: Prayer of St. Anselm. 3

The Lord's Prayer Modified traditional version (ASB). 4

Morning Canticles *Venite* and *Jubilate* Text ECUSA, see above. *Benedicite* Text CCP. 5 *Te Deum* and *Benedictus* Text ELLC. 6

Evening Canticles Text ELLC. 6

Easter Anthems 1 Corinthians 5:7-8; Romans 6:9–11, 1 Corinthians 15:20–22. Text ASB. 4

Gloria in Excelsis Text ASB. 4

Justorum Autem Animae Wisdom 3:1–8. Text CCP. 5

Salvator Mundi Based on a nineteenth-century original. Text ASB. 4

Manifestum Est 1 Timothy 3:16. Text CCP. 5

Glory: Early Christian Prayers, ed. A. Hamman, tr. W. Mitchell (Longman, 1967).

The Divine Praises Text CCP. 5

"In times of pain and grief . . ." from *Julian of Norwich's A Revelation of Love*, ed. M. Glasscoe (University of Exeter Press, new edition, 1993). Used with permission.

"The cross is the way of the lost . . ." Source not traced.

Celtic Journey Blessing Carmina Gadelica, Carmichael, Vol. III, p. 181; *Celtic Prayer for Protection*. Ibid., p. 65. Used by permission of Scottish Academic Press.

Collect for Purity Text ASB. 4

The Yoke of Obedience: The Methodist Service Book (1975), © Trustees for Methodist Church Purposes. Used by permission of Methodist Publishing House.

Additional Psalms Text ECUSA, see above (p. 143).

Psalm 23, Prayer Book Version From the Book of Common Prayer (1662).

Nocte Surgentes Office hymn, sixth century. *English Hymnal* (EH) 165.

Christ Whose Glory Charles Wesley. EH 258, *Hymns A & M New Standard* (AMNS) 4.

St. Patrick's Breastplate Version by Mrs. C. F. Alexander. EH 212.

Veni Sancte Spiritus Version by J. M. Neale. EH 155.

Veni Creator Spiritus Version by John Cosin. EH 153, AMNS 93.

O King Enthroned on High Greek, eighth century. Version by J. Brownlie. EH 454, AMNS 158.

Phos Hilaron Greek, third century. First version by John Keble (AMNS 8). Second version by Paul Gibson is copyright and used with permission.

Evening Hymn St. Mary's Abbey, West Mailing, Kent. Copyright, used with permission.

ABOUT PARACLETE PRESS

Who We Are

Paraclete Press is an ecumenical publisher of books and recordings on Christian spirituality. Our publishing represents a full expression of Christian belief and practice—from Catholic to Evangelical, from Protestant to Orthodox.

Paraclete Press is the publishing arm of the Community of Jesus, an ecumenical monastic community in the Benedictine tradition. As such, we are uniquely positioned in the marketplace without connection to a large corporation and with informal relationships to many branches and denominations of faith.

We like it best when people buy our books from booksellers, our partners in successfully reaching as wide an audience as possible.

What We Are Doing

Books

Paraclete Press publishes books that show the richness and depth of what it means to be Christian. Although Benedictine spirituality is at the heart of all that we do, we publish books that reflect the Christian experience across many cultures, time periods, and houses of worship.

We publish books that nourish the vibrant life of the church and its people—books about spiritual practice, formation, history, ideas, and customs.

We have several different series of books within Paraclete Press, including the bestselling *Living Library* series of modernized classic texts; *A Voice from the Monastery*—giving voice to men and women monastics about what it means to live a spiritual life today; award-winning literary faith fiction; and books that explore Judaism and Islam and discover how these faiths inform Christian thought and practice.

Recordings

From Gregorian chant to contemporary American choral works, our music recordings celebrate the richness of sacred choral music through the centuries. Paraclete is proud to distribute the recordings of the internationally acclaimed choir Gloriæ Dei Cantores, who have been praised for their "rapt and fathomless spiritual intensity" by *American Record Guide*, and the Gloriæ Dei Cantores Schola, which specializes in the study and performance of Gregorian chant. Paraclete is also the exclusive North American distributor of the recordings of the Monastic Choir of St. Peter's Abbey in Solesmes, France, long considered to be a leading authority on Gregorian chant performance.

Learn more about us at our Web site:
www.paracletepress.com, or call us toll-free at
1-800-451-5006.

The Little Book of Hours
Praying with the Community of Jesus
256 pages
ISBN: 1-55725-343-9
$13.95, Trade Paper

At the Church of the Transfiguration in Orleans, Massachusetts, the Liturgy of the Hours is celebrated every day by members of the Community of Jesus, an ecumenical Christian community. *The Little Book of Hours* presents a modified version of the offices used by the Community of Jesus, including four weeks of services, with three services for every day. This beautifully presented book (which includes a perforated bookmark) invites us to join with countless abbeys, churches, and individuals throughout the world who practice the Liturgy of the Hours.

The St. Francis Prayer Book
A Guide to Deepen Your Spiritual Life
Jon M. Sweeney
144 pages
ISBN: 1-55725-352-8
$13.95, Trade Paper

Jon M. Sweeney helps readers to kindle their prayer life with the words, guidance, and spirit of Francis of Assisi. This warm-hearted little book is a window into the soul of St. Francis, one of the most passionate and inspiring followers of Jesus.

"A beautiful selection of prayers in keeping with the spirit of St. Francis of Assisi."—*The Arkansas Democrat Gazette*

"This attractively presented little book is truly pocket-sized and portable, but full of rich content. . . . To spend a week using these daily offices can only deepen one's appreciation for the spiritual depth of . . . St. Francis."—*The Living Church*

Available from most booksellers or through Paraclete Press:
www.paracletepress.com;
1-800-451-5006.
Try your local bookstore first.